POLITICS and THE POLITICAL

THE GAME FOR POWER

by

M.A.N.ESQUIVEL.

index

prologue

The following text aims to introduce the main issues related to politics as a human activity. Politics is an activity propagated in our lives, even the people most reluctant to take an interest in politics are confronted on a daily basis with the measures and decisions taken by political actors that directly or indirectly affect our lives.

This book attempts a complete view of the political phenomenon, explaining its origins and evolution over time, making appropriate references to the present. Who should   read this book? The topics I address here are relevant to anyone interested in politics and government.

This is why I have tried to minimize specialized academic jargon as much as possible and keep the words and information as clear and concise as possible. I am not trying to boast of any specialized knowledge.

Above all, with regard to access to power, however, we cannot limit ourselves to observing this phenomenon from the point of view of access to power without all its variants.

This is what is the same and the text dealt with foreign policy, the economy, administration, leadership and   ethics. To be able to inform concepts that are part of politics and governments.

I have also addressed that it is a constitution, what it serves, its history and evolution over time and how the constitution is fundamental in our lives and in the conjunctural moment that we are living, without counting trying to answer the most common doubts of people who are related to the fundamental carta.

"Men make their own story"

CHAPTER 1

Politics and politics

Pretending to understand politics from scratch is a very pretentious thing. However, it is essential to take the first step in order to understand and give it the place it deserves which is a daily human activity.

At first glance the field of politics can be seen as an area whose boundaries have been established over centuries of discussion, practice and reflection.

To quote Hanna Arendt "where   men live together in society, in a civilizing sense, there is and always has been politics". (Hanna Arendt, p. 68).

But if we can see it from the side of society there will always be disparity of thoughts and influences, dominating and dominated.

This leads to the space of politics where the different "tensional forces" that occur in society are reflected, that is why we can say that: "politics is both the origin and the source of conflicts, but also as a way to resolve them and seek consensus to solve them. ",

From the point of view of science, politics seeks more prevention than predict. It is by e this, which differs from economics, sociology and even anthropology.

From the course of history, and citing in a way of example Plato, Machiavelli, Hobbes or Bobbio, in an attempt it was sought to found the bases of a science that prevented the most primitive and common actions that man performed while in society to be able to obtain power and to be able to preserve it.

For these great characters and authors of the story the first and most important, concern was dissolution, emptiness, chaos, anarchy, a king without crown, which may or may not be legitimate. This situation was simply distressing for the vast majority of the population. Chile also went through this situation called anarchy that lasted7 years.

Therefore, we could summarize this is a simple mathematical equation:

POLITICS= EXERCISEIO OF THE POWER- PUBLIC INTEREST – ORDER.

1- Exercise of power: it is the ability to influence the behavior of others.
2- Public interest: it is the area or sphere where policy is most effectively developed.
3- Order: absence of conflict, in other words, the vacuum of authority (without connotation of ideology or some style of regime).

Another definition of politics is from the historian Finley specializing in ancient Greece, who says that politics is the art of arriving at decisions through a civilized public discussion and then obeying such decisions as a necessary condition for the social presence of civilized men, his most notable work was ancient economics.

CHAPTER 2

Origins

The origin of the politics we know lies in the intersection of two worlds. On the bridge from the west to the east. The territory, although not the present country, neither the Staten or the nation, known as Greece.

By this I do not mean that in the East or in America politics was not practiced as such, as a human activity, but it was Greece that approached politics as something understandable to the human intellect, something that must be explained to the exception of nature or the gods.

In that ancient and distant Greece, the space of politics was reserved only to free men, moreover, the authentic content and the very meaning of politics was freedom in the polis, the man free from the shackles of the productions of goods, only reserved for slaves and metecos (foreigners), and freedom to understand about the affairs of the city.

The so-called political freedom in the Greek world was synonymous with equality "between equals" before the law (but in reality, this was very unequal, by the way, since it did not contemplate women, nor foreigners, nor slaves). To represent this equality there was a widely used word, which was "isonomy" the notion of isonomy comes from the Greek language. The term was used to refer to equality before the laws.

Isonomy means that citizens have the same political and civil rights. In this way it is an essential signal of a democratic regime.

The sophistics

The sophists, staunch enemies of Socrates and Plton, "merchants and relativists" of knowledge were the first to free politics from nature and the supernatural.

They disclosed and emphasized that politics had a weapon and this was discourse, which constituted a human sphere.

This happened to the vastness and extent of the Greek territory, in small towns called "Polis", composed of small populations, in slave economies with a select group of citizens who were dedicated to debating and managing the public space of the polis.

The sophists, are mostly foreigners who did not intervene in public affairs of the Athenian poly (in which this refers that they did not vote in the assemblies, nor did they hold public office) even when this was not a brake on their public appearances, in which they exploited all their discursive rhetoric capacity.

The founders of politics

Speaking of founders there are two great exponents and creators of the origin of classical politics, such as Pbrassand Aristotle.

Plato what he did was, personify Socrates, was a recognized and prolific author who dedicated several chapters to the constitution of the polis. For Socrates, the order of a society came from the subordination of the lower to the higher, as well as from the guidance of the king, the classical philosopher who held the title of statesman, since he knew the idea of the good.

Plato in an innocent way, thought and believed that power was not compulsive but quite the opposite that sought to enlighten men that it was good and virtuous.

His experience of experiencing this belief was a fiasco, as he attempted to cultivate Dionysius, tyrant of Syracuse. This character nearly ends the life of Pbrass, who had to escape to protect himself.

His key work in the world of politics is "The Republic", a writing that gives an account of the perfect city, in every sense, from its conformation, the division of tasks to its architectural design.

In reality, this city design is a brilliant and attractive utopia which, quickly, became an authoritarian nightmare, since as it happens in any conflict the dissonant elements were eliminated of rennet.

Aristotle was one of the other great exponents of Greek culture with great influences in the world of ideas. He is recognized for having influenced both Arabs and Christians alike, this can be demonstrated, as he was the teacher of the great Alexander the Great.

For Aristotle, the polis was the supreme community coexistence mode, thanks to the affective and justice alliance that united men.

Aristotle defined men as a zoon politikon, i.e., a "political animal", this phrase did not refer to the foreigners of the time who were considered barbarians. Aristotle defined and distinguished political regimes for the first time as a type and model because of the number of rulers and their purity, he believed that those who exercised power for their own benefit were impure.

The [1]Politeia, was a regime that, on the one hand, would be our current democracy, or rather in other words a political regime with legal institutions; secondly, the Politeia would be constituted by the "middle ground", that is to say not by the extremes of the polis, something like the middle class, although delimited to the citizens of the polis.

It was Aristotle who recovered the [2]Isonomic tradition which was fundamental in Athenian democracy, which had been overshadowed by the Platonic schools.

A criticism of Plato that did much to him both in antiquity and today, is that all those who imagine that the man representing the State, the king, the head of the family or father of the family and the owner of slaves are identical, do not express themselves

---

[1]Politeia: en a word that comes from the Greek that can be understood as the public space or simply public space. It is the space in which the city-state and the citizens converge. Plato and Aristotle's connotation for the word was that of an educated and participatory society.
[2]Isonomics: it comes from the Greek isonomikos and means "relative to equal law". Its lexical components are: isos (equal) and nomos (law), plus the suffix-ico (relative to).

properly, only see a difference of more or less in each of them and not a difference of species.

It is well known that the Greek world was absorbed by the nascent Rome, but its legacy extended beyond what was imagined thanks to its cultural richness and the spread of Alexander the Great.

The Romans subsumed politics to the [3]civitas. Cities grew in size, the economy became more complex, so it was necessary to replace politics with the legal order.

Cicero was a Roman politician and philosopher. He is considered one of the greatest Roman politicians (106 BC.C – 43 BC. C.) said that the civitas were not just any human aggregation but one based on the consensus of the law.

One of his most recognized phrases of Cicero was the people is not every set of men gathered in any way, but the whole of a multitude associated by the same right, which serves all equally.

In Rome the foundations of the republic are laid as a mode of government contrary to the monarchy, which is a forbidden word for the Romans.

This type of government, as is the republic seeks to balance the political forces that coexisting Roman cities. The image of the Roman circus is a mixture of social strata such as the plebe and patrician [4] families.

---

[3]Civitas: It is called Civitas to the legally organized citizen community based on the primacy of civil society (from which the development of the ius civile derives). The Roman civitas inherits the idea of Greek polis and was founded in 753 BC.C.

[4]Patrician families: the Patricians are those families upper class who influenced the independence of the nation (both for and against) and had culture, certain traditions and good

In the Middle Ages politics is the logicalized. With the debate of good and evil, which is linked to theological ethics. Saint Tomas, is the one who defines man as a "political and social animal", incorporating the idea of the social body, which is guided by Christian morality, which flourishes on earth.

However, from the beginning of the thirteenth century, the Middle Ages begins to crack in every aspect, political, with the questioning of the authority of the church in the government of men, economic, from the new lucrative emergency commercial, social activities, new customs break out and the strongly rooted, scientific ones are challenged, the geocentric system crumbles, with strong questions to the usefulness of the [5]Ptolemaic system.

It was a time when extreme problems can be said, solutions of equal intensity.

---

manners. In addition, these people considered '.'fathers of the fatherland'' had political and economic power.

[5] **Ptolismic:** From the geography of Ptolemy (second century), who considered the Earth as the center of the universe, around which all the stars moved

CHAPTER 3

The Awakening of Modernity

The age of modernity is considered the rupture of all the previous thing we knew about politics, the questioning that rose unchecked in the ancient Middle Ages.

However, modernity is more easily assimilated to the ancient world than what we know today, this is because national states did not exist, absolutism and wars were the order of the day, they were very common in those times. GDP per capital grew little and at a slow pace, and worse still, certain social fundamentals persisted that were difficult to change.

In this period or scenario, a Florentine character named Niccolò Machiavelli is born. Which was more learned by what he didn't say, than by what he wrote in his life. "The end Justifies the means", later became a classic in political analysis.

Niccolò Machiavelli was recognized for his main work, The Prince, is openly a plea for the exercise of raw and stark power.

The prince was written mainly to please the Medici family who had imprisoned him for alleged betrayals, he has a curious to say the least topicality referring to human behavior related to the exercise of power.

In this text he does not intend to paraphrase Machiavelli, although some phrases may be useful to know the spirit of this great work:

"... The things for which men are praised or censored, sin order to write something useful to those who understand it, I have had as more conducive to follow the real truth of matter than the ranted of the imagination in relation to it, because many imagined republics and principalities that were never seen or existed. There is so much distance between knowing how men live and knowing how they should live, to govern them, he abandons the study of what is done to study what would be most convenient to do, he learns rather what his ruin should do than what should preserve him from it... "(Machiavelli Nicholas, the Prince, Chapter XV).

About the prince it says:

"However, he must be more prudent in his reflections and in his actions, without feeding false imaginary fears, proceeding moderately and with humanity, so that overconfidence does not make him unwary and excess and distrust does not make him untouchable. From there arises a controversy, whether it is better to be loved than feared, and vice versa. It is answered that it would be appropriate to be one and the other, but since it is difficult to combine both, it is much safer and easier to be feared than loved when one of the two qualities is missing." (Machiavelli Nicholas, the Prince, Chapter XVII).

Machiavelli was the architect, unwittingly and opened a different world for the rule of men.

Machiavelli's attention was not on the constitution of the ideal or utopian city as the first founders of politics, nor on the good ruler, he had all his attention on the circumstances of the founding of cities specifically on their traditional political tradition.

He, too, was recognized by those who theologized and demoralized politics.

Machiavelli compared to other important figures in the world of politics, provided imprint to its essence as an activity that seeks to achieve, exercise and maintain power. Therefore, this means that men are fickle, unpredictable and fearful, politics does not have to be "dirty".

It is easier to eliminate the dissonant elements in the world of politics. There are very enriching contributions.

A major transformation occurs thanks to the Protestant Reformation. Of Martin Luther, and later Calvin, which were the promoters and defenses the idea of the inner dialogue between the individual and the divinity, through the "unintroverted" interpretation of the word sacra.

The reformation assented, unexpectedly, by a great unpublished invention that would change the world, the Gutenberg press.

In this way, in a slow but growing way, the divine presentation that was the press on earth helped to stipulate what was right, what the scriptures said, etc.) with this event, the stage of individual freedom of conscience was fatally wounded.

With a claim for religious tolerance, a new scale of a rational nature originates, [6]"iusnaturalism". The seventeenth century gave rise to natural law.

Of course, this for brevity this due to the most significant contributions, among them, the [7]contractualists (Hobbes, Locke

---

[6]**Iusnaturalism:** it is a philosophical and legal doctrine through which norms or rights are considered to be typical of the nature of the human being and prior to any established right. They are part of natural law.

[7]**Contractualists:** it is a modern current of political philosophy and law, which explains the origin of society and the State as an original contract between humans, by which a limitation of

and Rousseau) who very originally conceived a "rational and timeless" foundation to the origin of the Estate and society. These same characters placed in a hypothetical way, an intellectual innovation of the time which was based on assumptions, the existence of a social contract that did not depend on any divine or superhuman institution, but on the consensus of its associates.

From hobbes' pessimism, masterfully illustrated in the phrase "homo homini lupus" this phrase referred to, man is the wolf of man. This sentence meant that it bequeathed to man, through the fear of death and paradoxically, the consensus, a strong and omnipotent Estate, to Rousseau and his enunciation of the general will as recovery of the community among men, to the English Locke who proclaimed a limited Estate which would be divided in its functions in order to defend honor, property and life.

It was modernity that gave[8] autarky, independence and self-sufficiency to politics as an activity centered on the exercise of power, order and interference in public affairs different, although by over of the private sphere.

All of the above is politics, which broke away from Morality and Religion, and took over the State.

The twentieth century brought the exercise of politics into the sphere of power of the State, understood as a bureaucratic and professional entity.

---

freedoms is accepted in exchange for laws that guarantee the perpetuation and certain advantages of the social body.

[8]**Autarky: System** economic in which a state is supplied with its own resources, avoiding as much as possible imports.

CHAPTER 4

Polity and power

State is, quite simply, coercion. He imposes himself and exercises his authority over others, and it was the policy that gave him the theoretical and practical foundation of exercising power and domination in a broad way.

when it did not even exist as a formal bureaucracy as it is known today, the impersonations of state axis the power in the abundant eastern and Roman cities, con forms of provocative governments.

The highest authority that exercises the Estado, has different origins one of them is St. Augustine which indicated that God had created a temporary power to manage public affairs, the contractualists place it in a kind of imaginary pact, but to found it and to give it authority and legitimacy.

Economist Mancur Olson says that, in the past, there were certain gangs of wandering thieves who were hired by the villagers to rob them for an entire year, in exchange for protection and security against nearby enemy gangs.   In other words, one of the first mafias originated.

Throughout the history of man, the States had different forms of government such as: Empires, Absolutist Monarchies, Parliamentary, Republican and Democratic, but it was Max Weber, in the twentieth century, who most broadly and specifically defined the States:

"... an association of an institutional type, which the interior of a territory has successfully tried to monopolize physical and legitimized coercion as an instrument of domination, and brings together to that object the material means of exploitation in the hands of its directors, but having expropriated for them all the officials of autonomous class, who previously depended on those in their own right, and placing itself, in their place, at the supreme top". (Weber Max, economics and society, economic culture fund, pp. 1043–1076).

Weber also described how the exercise of power was related to certain characteristics of historical and social domination, traditional domination, based on custom, as well as by very elementary and quasi-irrational patterns of coexistence of charismatic domination, based on the personality of the leader of a very unstable character and, finally, legal rational domination, is based on legal and technical principles.

It is this latter type of domination that gives stability to the modern state and bureaucracy that we know today, and that is its raison d'être.

However, the Estado and the absolute exercise of power, aroused from early on serious misgivings among the most modern thinkers.

There is something that we must always remember that politics as a science is nothing more than preventive, not predictive and several well-known authors decided that it was their duty to reflect, and above all to make us reflect on the power of the State.

In particular, Montesquieu raised the need to divide the power of the State into three spheres in order to promote a policy of brakes and counter-weights.

The powers to which we refer are: the executive, legislative and judicial the division of powers was implemented after the independence of America one of its greatest examples the American colonies today United States, emancipated from the British crown.

Montesquieu's phrase on the policy of brakes and against weights is intended to shorten the power of the State or. For as James Madison (American politician and fourth U.S. president) said in The Federalist "... what is government but the greatest of reflections on human nature? If men were angels, no kind of government would be necessary. If the angels were to rule all men, there would be no need for internal and external controls of the government" (The Federalist, various editions).

From the most economic point of view, the power of the State has also interfered and decisively influenced the lives of human beings, as is evident when reference is made to the so-called political numbers, that is to say numbers that have been I do not know if manipulated, but distorted by the authority to favor some sector of the population.

This adage that I leave below serves to reflect, "you can do everything, except avoid the consequences", this adage wants to tell us something very simple and easy to understand that all our actions have consequences and as Newton's third law would say for all action there is an equal and opposite reaction.

Over the centuries there have been authors who, by dint of work and interpretations has been able to analyze different types of State: The State absolutist (xvi and xvii centuries), the Estado liberal (xviii and XIX centuries), the Estado interventionist (which is in the decade of the 30), the State of welfare (from the Second World War), the State neoliberal (from the decade of the 90) which for many supposedly is in crisis.

In historical precedents on the State, it is somewhat capricious, biased, generalist.

If each of the aforementioned State ever came into existence, they most likely did so simultaneously and it is hardly possible to box it in or identify it beyond a reliable representative.

It is more interesting and enriching to study and analyze such historical perspectives from the specific historical events that took place, as well as from the materials and intellectuals that made this State a fundamental actor, with a certain historical identity.

In conclusion, the writer F. Hölder Lin should be mentioned:

"What has made the state   a hell on earth has been precisely, Man trying to make it a heaven or a paradise on earth."

CHAPTER 5

The Government

There are times when the terms State and Government are used indiscriminately, however, they have different meanings and connotations.

The State is continuous uninterruptedly, my entry that governments meet a cycle that varies according to the system of government of the day or in force.

Systems of government can be authoritarian or democratic. Among the latter are governments that are: presidentialism, semi-presidentialism and parliamentarians.

Throughout the American continent the presidential system prevails, the power falls on the executive (president and cabinet), the legislative power (Parliament) and the judiciary (justice), the first two powers such as the executive and the legislative are legitimized by periodic elections.

On the other hand, the European continent is dominated by semi-presidential and parliamentary systems, in which Parliament has greater and strong influence in the formation of cabinets.

The duration of the different forms of government can range from 4 to 6 years, and in certain government positions there is a possibility of re-election of the authorities. In the particular case of Chile, the government has a duration of 4 years, and the executive without the possibility of immediate re-election, and in other government positions there is the possibility of re-election of maximum two terms.

The traditional idea of power is that it is distributed from the top down, from the state to society, from the power of the church to its parishioners, from the leader to its followers, from the teacher to the student, from the doctor to the patient, etc.

However, Michel Foucault had the sagacity or vision to propose the existence of a microscopic power, which was almost capillary, atomic, disseminated by the rest of society.

The microphysics of power crosses the bodies imposing, often inconsequently, the designs of the power of the day with force so that it is considered as a natural mandate.

Microscopic power relations are scattered among families and friends, sexual and reproductive customs, all these examples I have just mentioned play a conditioning and conditioning role.

Foucault's contribution was very important, which had a double contribution: one was to take power off the cusp, and the second was to show that this dissemination is economic, since it is more convenient to watch than punish, and in this way the bodies behave all the time like the cusp.

This new notion of power is complemented by another statement, that knowledge is power and vice versa, and this helps to spread power unconsciously.

CHAPTER 6

The Political Ideological Doctrines

Nowadays it is difficult to break with certain traditions of classifying politicians, their actions and the structures that accompany them as "left" or "right", even if they rarely behave like one or the other.

The classification that we allude to today of "left" or "right" was born around 1788-17789 when the French Generals met, and to the left of the King sat the representatives of the third Estado commonly "the people", but at that time known as the "plebe" and, on the right side, were the privileged who were the nobility and the clergy.

Even at that time the flourishing bourgeoisie was located in the social stratum belonging to the commoners.

This classification persisted over time and it was established that the left had an economically redistributive and egalitarian inclination, while the right, pejoratively, was associated with the liberation of the market and the protection of private property from state interference.

In a somewhat briefly incomplete way, we could say that:

And, anarchism? Or[9]anarcho-capitalism? and what happens with religious fundamentalisms? ecological movements, anti-

---

[9]Anarcho-capitalism: it is a current that proposes the elimination of the state as an economic agent, the total suppression of the taxation, while advocating for the free market, private property and condemns fraud.

globalization, or the very current "indignados"? and our precious and eternal Latin American populism? Is the latter right or left?

As you can see the classification is completely arbitrary and biased, as it could well be a liberal to completely disagree or identify him with a conservative or a Nazi, fascist.

Also, a Marxist-Leninist to be in total opposition with a [10]Maoist, a [11]Trotskyist, even with a [12]Stalinist, etc. On the other hand, one could say that the Peron of 1946 is completely different from that of the 70s. As far as we can tell, there are countless confusions.

That is why it is urgent for political science to modify the classification that has been used to date, and to promote one that is less pre judicious, more expeditious and flexible.

In this text we are not trying to solve it, but to make visible the variants that exist.

A possible variant could be the proposal postulated by Friedrich Hayek which saw the political doctrines in a particular way, concisely explained, there are three ideological, doctrinal aspects most important all in a black color.

1- Conservatism: this position relates to the maintenance of traditions, and is directly related to the homeland, economic

---

[10]Maoist: it focuses on revolutionary mass mobilization with independent industries created throughout the country, providing the Chinese population with the necessary resources to live and weapons.

[11]Trotskyite: it is a current of Marxism developed largely by Leon Trotsky. In general terms, it represents a contrast to Stalin's vision of Marxism-Leninism and its theories of socialism in a single country.

[12]Stalinist: is a political current derived from the model of government applied by Joseph Stalin in the Soviet Union. Responds to Stalin's interpretation of Marxism

protectionism, religion, limited rights, authority based on customs and hierarchical leadership without question.

2- Socialism: the post-socialism is related to the commitment to the ideas of community and equality.

3- Liberalism: liberalism is the defender of the free market, the non-interference of individual rights by the state and respect for the individual rights of man.

Among the aforementioned doctrines different variants are formed, according to specific circumstances of the political system, for example, these circumstances are created when different alliances are formed between the various sectors, to maintain the status quo, so of assumption we will say and describe some cases, liberalism approaches and becomes conservative for example populism in 1946 and in the 90s, in others it is socialism that becomes conservative, another case would be Stalinism, Korea, Cuba, or the populism of 2010 of Venezuela and Argentina, and also socialism approaches liberalism when dressed in the social democratic clothes Europe.

Anarchists, liberals, socialists, conservatives and environmentalists fluctuate between socialism and liberalism.

In any case, it must be understood that this distinction encompasses certain political traits, theileriid of power, public interest and order, only, relates to the moment and some measures directed towards society.

In terms of economics, that is to say politics, economics is in the background, except perhaps for private property.

There are several variants that seek to replace the outdated model that classifies left and right.

In any case, there is nothing to overcome the old model of political scheme.

We are living in times of change, there are supposed apathies in general and there are parties that can be said to catch everything that only want the largest number of voters in the middle for their ends, so why not update these partisan schemes and avoid further confusion?

CHAPTER 7

democracy

To begin by talking about democracy I want to begin by quoting Winston Churchill "... democracy is the worst form of government, except for all the other forms that have been tested from time to time."

The first antecedent or the Cuna of democracy is, ancient Greece.

Around the fifth century BC.C, the Greek polis constituted small socio-economic unit's cities Estates, as mentioned above, the polis allowed men over 20 years with the conditions of free men and as citizen polis in this category did not enter neither slaves, nor foreigners, nor women, regardless of social status, participated actively and fully in the government of the polis.

A prominent Athenian politician and ruler Clysters was a reformer who managed to introduce a participatory constitution in 507 BC.C, in that constitution a system of elections of authorities was proclaimed and instituted, composed of an abbreviated form, in a kind of assembly known at that time [13]Ekklesia which was constituted of several hundred thousand citizens who elected a council of 500 citizens who, in turn, elected a committee of 50 men, which had the mission of guiding the proposals made by the council.

---

[13]Ekklesia:era the main assembly of Athenian democracy in classical Greece.

As can be seen, the system of the time does not concentrate power in a single person, but we can verify that the power was in the participation, although limited, of the members of the city state.

As in any democracy, the Athenian was not without errors in its operation.

To name a few facts, Athenian democracy was restored, after a string of 30 tyrants, which was directly responsible for the trial against Socrates, who was a mentor of Pbrass, the accusation was for having corrupted the youth with teaching against the gods, although a more logical reason would be that the philosopher had ridiculed more than one powerful.

As we can already see in previous paragraphs, for Aristotle democracy was an impure form of government for trying to respond to the interests of the majority, its form was the least impure of all, according to him even though his form of governance was the most tyrannical.

Democracy was, or is still in danger, of overflowing into a suede demagoguery, which in turn could be transformed into tyranny.

Aristotle rescued or the incorporation of social economic interests, which were always in conflict, which allowed democracy and proposed it in an ideal way the Politeia. About the latter it was said "... that it is not in any way the poor than the rich, but that both classes are alike" (Aristotle, various editions, politics).

In our time there is little left of such a distant democracy, perhaps only the idea that was direct, something that is not very clear either, but it can be said that its influence has been notorious for our way of governing, but this type of democracy is more recognized for its legacy than for a model to be imitated.

Modern democracy after the experience of Greek democracy, there were few experiences that lived similar processes so long and effective. It must be recognized that for several centuries there was theological policy which stood   strongly as a guide route or compass over the fate of several generations.

After centuries of theological politics, new thinkers with new foundations had to be expected in order to move on to rational thoughts of the Renaissance in order for earthly governments to be formed.

The above did not mean that we became the democracy we know, but rather it took several more centuries for it to be channel led into today's democracy.

During the nineteenth century democracy underwent transformations or a kind of metamorphosis as a form of containment for the more affluent social strata, which originated a restricted democracy, but as the working masses make more noise in the political scenario, it is distinguished that it was not only necessary but also understandable the participation and incorporation of these new and powerful actors of society.

The new mass democracy was becoming more and more entrenched in the world of politics, its new procedures and prospects for survival were growing more and more.

When this new kind of democracy was accepted in the twentieth century, it had to suffer blows from totalitarian ideologies, which sought to be responsible for crises and wars, these ideologies were Nazism, Fascism and Stalinism.

These ideologies were strongly conservative and nationalist, which sought to vindicate a past of pride.

It is difficult to account for the historical direction of democracy, there is no linear narrative, only a long line of events that account for the intrinsic weakness of citizen participation.

Robert Dahl, has been able to synthesize the modern democracy in an effective and detailed graphic.

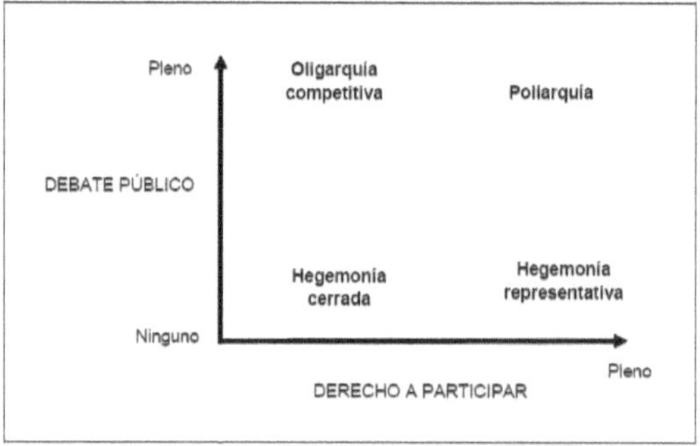

The transformation of democracy that we know today is due to three historical paths that helped to change in different measures the liberation or participation of man in politics.

1- One of the first nations to follow the path of modern democracy are the Anglo-Saxon countries, which evolved from authoritarianism to restricted democracy and then reached the modern

2- The second to follow this path was Latin America, and to a lesser extent European country.

3- And finally, a direct step extreme imposition as was Germany and Japan after the defeat of the Second World War, and the Arab countries enter this modern democracy in this century of change?

The most common polyarchies known in this text as modern democracy, is characterized by certain specific qualities, to name a few:

a) Resolving settlements peacefully
b) Social diversity
c) Freedom of expression (participation, expression, confession, etc.)
d) Political party systems
e) Periodic elections
f) Leadership renewal
g) Respect for rights
h) Design institutions according to the virtues mentioned

Today's democracies must respect to a greater or lesser extent, the qualities mentioned.

Currently, the democracy in which we live enjoys relative prestige worldwide, of course according to the political scientist Norberto Bobbio it presents some flaws, false promises, lack of citizen centrality, lobbying in interest groups, lack of participation, hidden issues in the governments of the day and an arbitrary system.

And all these failures to our democracy are caused by vices as they are, the technocracy that only serves the complexity of the affairs of governments, the bureaucracy this due to the growth of the State and the failure of its channels of operation and the resolution of conflict, poor performance due to the slowness and incapacity and the null response to social demands.

In another view, from the economist Joseph Schumpeter, followed by other analysts, which opened a side of economic analysis, which claimed that the market resembled democracy, voters with buyers, and politicians with sellers.

Schumpeter, has another look at politics, since he denies the existence of a common good and alludes to voters, rationally alluding that they have various alternatives as if it were a market.

The biggest problem that exists among voters to this day, is the asymmetric information which means that we do not really know what the government plan is, nor the intentions of the politician and that, once the candidate is chosen, it is necessary to wait a long period of time to choose another candidate.

Democracy was consolidated in the West throughout the twentieth century, at the beginning of this century in the United States and Northern Europe, in the 70s mainly Mediterranean Europe Spain, Portugal and Turkey. Latin America between the 80 and 90, ex-Soviet East Europe starting from the 90.

In the second decade of the twenty-first century, it experienced what was called the Arab Spring, with an outcome still uncertain, but with hope that it will reach a safe haven, for the good of all Arabs, particularly women.

In the political literature there is a wealth of information about the transition to democracy, this due to the passages of authoritarian governments or dictatorships that are then transformed into full or semi-full democracies.

The boundaries of transitions are blurred, they start when democratic and fair elections are held, but we don't know when they end.

One observation comes from our late trans-Andean political scientist Guillermo O'Donnell, who took on the task of observing the different democracies of Latin America and called them with a low level of institutionalist, since it lacked values and norms as democracies.

He found this low level, as he did not find the predominant traits that the [14]aforementioned polyarchies had to have.

Democracy will continue to vary as time and society progress, being a wide field of discussion thanks to the constant communication technology, and most regrettably, the apathy to participate in the most sublime the most beautiful thing that politics has the periodic elections which must be defended with cloak and sword.

---

[14]**Polyarchies:** Government that is exercised by many.

CHAPTER 8

Political Parties and Electoral Systems

Political parties are the indispensable vehicle for the ordinary citizen to participate in politics, and for politicians it is the vehicle for gaining power.

The emergence of political parties dates back to the mid-nineteenth century when political groups emerged that were born in the great cities of the world as in the United States or Europe, in Chile formal political parties would not appear before the public light until the mid-1850s, the emergence of a political system as such was the result of the politicization that lived Chile by conflict between the clerical and anticlerical the church conflict and Estado caused by the "question of the sacristan".

The historical evolution of the authorities of the day with the nascent political parties was not so direct, nor peaceful. But they had to tolerate other political ideological expressions and the second thing, those who held some kind of position against the government of the day, had to accept the rules of the game.

It could be taken as the origin of the formation of political parties to the Reform Act of 1832 in England, or other possible origins could be between the Federalists of Hamilton and Republicans of Jefferson in the United States, however, since its conception there were always different sides in conflicts such as Unitarian and Federalist examples in Argentina, pelucones and pipiolos in Chile.

Entering the political parties one of the most outstanding is the conservative party, which were increasingly isolated for representing the past, but to modernize and survive time they joined or merged the liberal parties, although in the end they embraced nationalism when they were threatened by the wave of workers' movements caused by the Russian revolution of the proletariat.

During the period of the world wars, and before the disastrous and disastrous experience of Japanese, Italian and Germination alism, the social democratic parties took on greater relevance until the 70s in the middle of the twentieth century

With the evolution of politics, the political parties took the logic of being like a broom, that is to say seek to capture the attention of the citizens, with proposals distant from the extremes.

Today the political parties continue with the same logic catching the attention of people through new communication technologies Sora they are: Twitter, Facebook, Instagram, among others.

Beyond the historical account and the nature of political parties, there is a kind of classification that was made, in the first instance by Maurice Duverger, in the 50s, and more contemporaneously by Giovanni Sartori. There are others, but these are the most relevant to understanding the political spectrum of any region or country.

	SITEMA DUVERGER	SARTORI SYSTEM
	Features	Features
TYPES OF PARTY SYSTEMS	QUANTITATIVE CLASSIFICATION	QUANTITATIVE CLASSIFICATION
ONE MATCH	ONE-PARTY	UNIQUE, HEGEMONIC, PREDOMINANT
TWO MATCHES	bipartisan	Bipartisan
MANY KICKS	multiparty	LIMITED, EXTREME OR POLARIZED, ATOMIZED

As we can see in the following table, the Duverger system is ranked according to the number of parties competing for power.

On the other hand, the system of Sartori, aims to make more exhaustive, since it distinguishes different historical forms all this in relation to political parties and their polarization this in cause, to the existence of three or more political parties with wide possibilities and that represent different visions and options of representation within the political spectrum.

	DUVERGER SYSTEM	SATORI SYSTEM
SYSTEM OF PARTIES	Features	Features
ONE-PARTYING	FORMER USSR AND CUBA	FORMER USSR AND KOREA OF NORETE
bipartisanship	USA, ENGLAND	USA, ENGLAND, HONDURAS URUGUAY
MUTIPARTISAN	FRANCE, ARGENTINA, GERMANY, ITALY	FRANCE, ARGENTINA, GERMANY, ITALY, CHILE, AMONG OTHERS

1- The single-party or one-party system, according to Sartori, is divided into three, taking into consideration whether there is competition or not and whether it governs a single ideology or official party, not tolerating other parties or opposition.

2- The classic two-party system is characterized by a type of alternation of power between two main parties. To name a few examples work and Conservatives in England or Republicans and Democrats in America. In this type of named system, parties lean toward the center of the political spectrum and their proposals differ little from each other.

3- Multipartyism is between a bipolar competition, that is to say it is a competition of several parties, but only two with possibilities.

   For example, pre-Nazi Germany was characterized by a multi-party system of extremes, highly polarized, with anti-system, anti-Semitic parties and promoters of violence.

The current Chilean electoral system is the D'Hondt method, the following system is a mathematical method for the allocation of [15]seats which allows to obtain the number of elected officials assigned to the candidacy, which is proportional to the number of votes received.

Example in a hypothetical case five political positions (X) are elected and three lists run to the election.

A) Of the 3 competing lists in which List A gets 100 votes, List B gets 60 votes and finally List C gets 40 votes.

---

[15] seat: A seat occupied by a politician in one of the parliamentary chambers.

B) Of which the total votes obtained by each list will be divided by the number of positions to be elected, i.e. by position 1, by position 2, by position 3, by position 4 and by position 5.

C) From the numbers resulting from this division are sorted in descending order up to the number of offices to be elected in each district. In the example the first 5 results.

D) The final order of the would be of charges:

1st Place 100 Votes (List A)

2 Ranked 60 Votes (List B)

3rd Place 50Votes (List A)

4th Place 40Votes (List C)

5th Place 33Votes (List A)

E) Elected candidates:

List A would get 3 positions

List B would get 1 position

List C would get 1 position

Important aspects to highlight

(a) The Quota Act, the total number of candidates for both deputies and senators registered by the political parties, as well as male and female candidates, may exceed 60 per cent, which ensures that at least 40 per cent will be of a different sex. Which will be applied in the parliamentary elections of 2017, 2021, 2025 and 2029.

b) Contributions by parliamentary candidates of 2017, 2021, 2025 and 2029, political parties will receive 500 promotion units for each elected candidate. In addition, the candidates of the Senate and the Chamber of Deputies will be entitled to an additional reimbursement of their electoral expenses of 0.0100 units of promotion for each vote obtained.

c) General data the Senate, 50 Senators are elected and each region corresponds to a Senatorial District of the country.

The Chamber of Deputies is elected 155 Deputies for the 28 existing districts.

CHAPTER 9

Politicians and the decision-making process

The image we have of politicians is recurrent due to the collective social imaginary, about what politicians do about the entire process of daily decision-making that they are confronted with.

This is due to the concept that has transcended politics and politicians, as an activity and profession, that is to say that of a person who is dedicated to good governance.

Politicians assume so much relevance and make it felt within their own speeches which are full of good intentions and remain in their good intentions, this demonstrated in their actions in office since it is very different from the image they projected in their speeches.

The politician and his political activity are closer to the reality posed by Machiavelli than that posed by Plato and Aristotle who postulated good government.

It should be remembered that Machiavelli described politics as an activity as having the purpose of seeking, exercising and maintaining power.

This is nothing more because politics is not moral, but there is its own morality of politics.

To quote the words of Max Weber, "He who seeks the salvation of the soul, his own and of others, must not seek it in the path of politics, because the various tasks of politics can only be solved by violence". (Max Weber, science and politics, "politics as a profession", ed. various).

This is because the political career gives a sense of power.

The feeling of exerting an influence on men, the feeling of participating in the power that is inflicted on them and, above all, the awareness of having the hands important historical events.

What is at stake in political activity, power, history, economic resources, influence on the behavior of others.

State is the sand, the place where bids for the rawest power are solved. Even though the type of confrontation has changed over time, and the physical confrontations that put the lives of politicians at stake no longer exist or decline, there is a constant struggle for power.

As we already know politics is an activity propagated in our lives and we could go so far as to say that we are all casual politicians and this would be reflected when we vote, we express our opinion and we participate, however, there is a special class of politicians, and it is those who live for politics, or who live off politics who do not live up to their position, since politics is a non-minor distension.

Politicians must be classified into two types, namely those who live for politics and those who live on politics.

Politicians who live **for** politics have, in some way, income or income outside politics, and only use politics to provide a greater network of contacts and influences.

Politicians who make a living **from** politics are dependent on variants of politics and have their ups and downs when governments change.

The latter case of politicians, in general, have an aspiration that is that of service living for politics, and at best, they become just good civil servants.

The secret of the politician is to remain in his possession, and not to be exposed, but to make use of his contacts to continue clinging to his positions.

The weapons of a politician are the speech, the influences they can exert on others and the media and social networks. Their enemies are a lack of management, control and charisma.

It is for the same reason that there are intellectual currents that insist on the need to strengthen institutions or entities with norms, objectives and values that curb the personal ambitions of those who live to exercise power.

Politicians who aspire to live for politics must ensure four virtues, influence, pragmatism, substantial incomes, and low budget constraints.

CHAPTER 10

Politics

Politics is a service activity whose main objective is to resolve differences peace full Yan reasonably between individuals and human groups in society. More   precisely, politics is a particular way of dealing with conflicts, which must be resolved democratically. There are many areas of our lives where politicians do not act, but what are these areas? they are all those in which logic is not democratic.

Politics only makes sense because human beings live in community, in the same space where interaction is not allowed to be subject to any norm other than that of free discussion, and social projects have different objectives of reaching agreements that make possible the coexistence of diverse thoughts and conflicts. Politics cannot seek to eliminate social conflicts, but to make it more livable.

A more accepted definition of social conflict is that offered by sociologist Lewis Closer, citing it as "struggle for values and power or scarce resources, in the course of which opponents wish to neutralize or eliminate their rivals at all costs." The previous quote is of a harsh characteristic, since it says and paraphrases it talks about hurting or even eliminating rivals. It is a definition that, in practice, is an affirmation not only about the situation, but about the way in which they will inevitably end up resolving it, by means of elimination.

Maybe it's the best definition, the way it most closely resembles our reality, the way we normally live or think. Conflict is a painful situation, in which confrontation is inevitable, where there is much more at stake than victory or defeat, since what wins can only come from the loss of the other, however, this is the only most accurate definition of conflict that we can find in the sociological literature.

Max weber postulates another definition no less classical than that of Lewis Coser, which he says characterizes conflict as that action that is intentionally oriented to the realization of the will of the main actor against the resistance of the other party or more parties that could exist, without substantially modifying the substance of the previous definition, two or more opposing parties, which is a characterization that does not prejudge the outcome of the conflict, and it is for this very reason that it is milder, although we know or can assume that in most situations it will be almost impossible to peacefully carry out the will of one of the parties in question over the other party that exists.

Anthony Giddens is the renowned author of the sociology manual in which he describes the following definition of conflict, "antagonism between the various individuals in society". This definition at first glance seems very simple, it is a self-referential definition that therefore does not define anything.

However, it is this same simplicity that gives interest to the definition proposed by Giddens, is there conflict when and why? There is conflict when there is an antagonist at the heart of the system, and it is this antagonist that is different from any complex social reality.

The important thing is not the existence of the conflict, since the conflict is always in our lives is in our social reality, it is the perspective of the conflict in which we develop the definition, it is the approach we make to understand it.

If we can conceive the situation of conflict in a type of interference that affects our social stability, that generates ruptures of our normality or threat to order, our first reaction as human beings will be to deny it, hide it or definitively eliminate it.

We identify conflict as aggression, to the point that we seek and will look for causes and causes, and especially the assumptions responsible for these conflicts, of which others will always be the cause never ourselves. Then we intend to neutralize, harm or eliminate our rivals as they never existed, whom we will point out and disqualify as public enemies, when in fact they are nothing else as antagonists, companions, citizens of the same history, convections of the same language, of the same history, race of inhabitants of the same complex reality.

Political power is a consequence of the exercise of functions by persons holding representative and popular office within a political system of a country.

Political power is a democratic system with division of powers within a country, as are the executive and legislative, while the third power is the judiciary, it is within a different system since its legitimacy is not guaranteed by the vote like the other powers mentioned, but by the faithful fulfillment of their functions and convictions.

Political power must be legitimized when it is elected according to the laws of a country through its constitution. In democratic countries, it is based on the legitimacy granted by its own people through popular voting through periodic elections.

Political power is abusive when its leaders exceed the exercise of their functions, when in matters within the scope of the other powers. Political power is illegitimate when methods or mechanisms not authorized by law are used and governmental power is seized and attributed, without having the legitimacy of the popular vote.

CHAPTER 11

Organization of powers

To begin with, what is power? Power means the power to command and to be obeyed, but in the field of politics itis the activity of the State. Which changes its definition to public power as the ability of the State to compel someone to perform a certain act.

Public power is fundamental to the functioning of a country and to the people who inhabit it, because it is these same people who live together in the same physical space. It is for this reason that an order and establishment of rules that allow healthy human coexistence is required, which translates into the exercise of power.

In all society groups are formed, which create a center of power which diversifies in various directions such as: religion, economy, culture and even fashion. Society could be seen as a constellation of powers, but all these aforementioned powers are concentrated in a single organization, which allows harmony to flow in the different strata of society, which produces the integration of political power into one.

Power is born as a need to ensure human coexistence, therefore, if there were no order and authority, which is distributed as equitably as possible, which would make it impossible to live together and interact in a society capable of reaching the category of State.

In general, public power is usually used in a plural form "public powers", which is thus used because of its meaning as a set of governmental bodies and institutions. These institutions are grouped into three different powers: the legislative, executive and judicial.

Separation of powers, this theory of separation was common among various thinkers of the eighteenth century, which was enunciated during the time of the enlightenment, some of its representatives are: Alexander Hamilton, John Locke, Jean-Jacques Rousseau and Montesquieu. These great illustrators had different nuances.

According to the vision of the enlightenment, the Estate exists for the sole purpose of protecting man from other men. Man for his safety is able to sacrifice complete freedom for the security of not being affected in the right to life, integrity, liberty and private property. It is in this way that legitimacy is given to the public authority and its respective institutions.

However, on certain occasions man is already protected from his fellow man, but not from the State itself, which on specific occasions could oppress them, through the powers granted to him by the people themselves.

In the classical formulation, the Estate is considered to be the protector of the citizens, bound by the laws created by the legislature, but it is the executive that put them into practice in order to resolve conflicts. But the government administration that is in charge of supervising or enforcing the laws is the judiciary, which operates the old monopolizing regime in a single absolutist monarchical entity to which the practice of despotism is granted.

The legislature refers to one of the three primary powers of the State, together with the executive and the judiciary. The legislative branch is based on the adoption of regulations with the status of law.

The power of the State is divided into three traditional branches:

In a stable democracy, the legislature drafts and amends existing laws according to the impression and opinion of the citizens. Its specific function is to pass laws and is in charge of a deliberative body that can be the congress, parliament or house of representatives.

The primary powers and functions of the Executive are to enact and enforce laws usually adopted by the government or by the head of the State himself.

In the branch of political science and constitutional law, the executive is the highest branch of the State, responsible for the day-to-day management of government. In many countries, the word government is used to refer to the executive branch, but this is often confusing in an international context.

According to the theory of the separation of powers, it is the legislative branch that is responsible for drafting laws, but it is the task of the executive branch to interpret and standardize laws, and enforcing them is the sole task of the judiciary.

All the above mentioned of the separation of powers is what is carried out only on paper, because in practice this separation of powers is usually not absolute, since the head of government is the most visible figure intestate.

The judiciary is that power within the State, which is responsible for administering justice in society, through the application of legal norms, in the resolution of disputes.

Power itself takes on different meanings or definitions according to the public authority, is understood as an organization, institution or set of State bodies, which in the case of the judiciary are judicial or jurisdictional orders which are divided between courts and tribunals, which usually enjoy impartiality and autonomy.

In order to prevent one of the branches of power from becoming supreme, and to include it to cooperate, governmental systems that are employed in the separation of powers are typically created with a system called checks and balances in Spanish control and checks and balances that refers to various rules of procedure that allow one branch to limit to another.

The public power constitutes a legitimate legal capacity before the law and before the people, who possess the three political powers to be able to exercise effectively. Through the actions and tasks that are conferred by the constitution.

It is a mechanism designed to prevent the concentration of power in the same authority. By dividing power into different bodies, each of them controls that the others do not concentrate more powers than those established by law. That is why it is said that "power slows down power".

Constitutions generally distinguish three powers:

1) Legislative: power responsible for the creation, modification and repeal of laws.
2) Executive: it is the power in charge of executing and enforcing the law. Its main function is to lead the country politically and administer goods and services.
3) Judicial: it is the power responsible for resolving legal conflicts between individuals and the State and applying the law to the specific case.

All Chilean constitutions have recognized a division of powers. In order to give effect to the separation of powers, any constitution must establish at least.

Who is in charge of each power and how the authorities are elected the current Constitution establishes that the government and administration correspond to the President of the Republic, who shall be elected by universal suffrage by an absolute majority of the validly cast votes?

The powers and attributes of the authorities are article 24 of the Constitution that the authority of the President extends to all those aimed at the preservation of public order within and external security of the Republic. To this end, it has the special powers conferred on it by Article 32 of the Constitution, for example, to appoint ministers of State, or to declare constitutionally exceptional states or to prepare draft laws. For its part, the Constitution confers on the National Congress the power to make laws (article 63 of the Constitution) and on the courts the power to dispense justice (article 76 of the Constitution).

The way in which the authorities exercise their powers, the president of the Republic must act through supreme decrees, Congress through laws and the courts through rulings.

In fact, since the constitution lays down the powers of each power or body of the State, none of them may exercise the functions which correspond to the others.

That said, it is important to clarify that the separation of powers is not absolute. There is a global tendency for legislative function to be shared by Congresses with executive branches. In many constitutional systems, executive powers can also introduce bills. In any case, the essential thing is that these shared powers should be regulated in the Constitution.

As in other countries, the president has some legislative powers, such as introducing bills, establishing urgencies during their passage through Congress, or vetoing a bill passed by Congress. And since the constitutional reform of 1943 to the Constitution of 1925, only the president can present bills that involve expenses on the part of the state, a power that is also contemplated in the Constitution of 1980.

In relation to the distribution of powers, a constitution must also regulate the territorial structure of power. The constitution must define whether the country shall be a unitary State (an executive, legislative and judicial power for the whole territory) or a federal State (an executive, legislative and judicial power in each region plus a central executive, legislative and judicial power responsible for the issues common to the whole country).

CHAPTER 12

Fundamental rights

Fundamental rights arose in constitutionalism under the premise that there are rights inherent in our human nature. These are faculties that everyone as a person has for the sole reason of being human.

Constitutions do not create these rights, but recognize them, thus facilitating their legal and judicial protection. Example: we all have the right to physical integrity because we are human beings, not because the constitution creates the right. However, the constitution creates mechanisms for courts of justice to protect people from violations of my integrity by the State or by individuals.

Generally, rights are classified into two broad groups:

a) Classical rights
b) Social rights

Classical rights enclose the various rights such as freedom, civil and political. Which gave rise to constitutionalism. These are powers that essentially oblige the State to refrain from interfering in them. They involve areas of immunity, barriers to protection against the power of the State, which can be protected by the courts in the event of infringement.

The right to life implies that the state cannot deprive me of life. Freedom of conscience implies that the state cannot prevent me from expressing my beliefs. They also include rights that allow me to participate in public life: freedom of expression, of association, of assembly, the right to vote.

These classic rights include two that constitute guarantees of the other rights: Equality before the law and due process of law. Equality before the law means that the State cannot introduce arbitrary or capricious differences. Due process is a set of guarantees that ensures that no one can be deprived or limited in their rights but within the framework of a judicial procedure, observing certain rules such as the right to a defense, to have legal assistance, presumption of innocence, impartiality of the judge, etc.

The first constitutions only recognized classical rights. The rights of liberty can be invoked before a judge, even if they are only recognized in the constitution and there are no laws that develop them in detail.

Social rights Are a set of powers, principles and programmatic criteria in the field of social policy, the purpose of which is to improve the material living conditions of people and greater material equality.

As a rule, these rights are only incorporated into constitutions at the beginning of the twentieth century. Some are areas of immunity and protection in social matters, such as collective work rights (edging, collective bargaining and strike action) and the right to a pollution-free environment. Like classical rights, in principle these rights can be protected by the courts on the basis of their constitutional recognition alone.

Other social rights consist of benefits payable by the State, such as the right to health, the right to education, the right to social security, the right to housing. The realization of the latter requires the corresponding allocation of economic resources by the legislator, which will allow their possible judicial protection.

The 1980 Constitution recognizes some social rights such as the right to health, education or social security, but leaving the law its further development and implementation. For example, the regulation of the SAPRES, the AFP or the amount of social security contributions do not appear in the Constitution, but in different specific laws that can be modified by Congress.

While I cannot go to the judge to demand, for example, the coverage of a specific treatment invoking my right to health, I can demand that I not be discriminated against in the way public policies are applied in health matters. Example: The executive cannot propose a public policy that arbitrarily excludes treatment for a group of people.

CHAPTER 13

Chilean political system

The political regime or political system of a state, which involves the form of government of a country, such as the organization of public powers and their interrelations, socio-economic structures, traditions, customs and political forces that drive the work of institutions.

The most well-known classification of political regimes distinguishes between:

a) Autocratic regime which, in general terms, are those regimes where the rulers must first behave according to the rules which. They are divided into:

Totalitarian regime: Totalitarian rulers can participate in the political process through a single channel, which is guided by a totalitarian ideology that controls and regulates all aspects of people's lives. Minorities dissenting from the established decree are not allowed or tolerated. The ideal political party of government develops the instruction and dissemination that gives permanent support to the given regime.

Authoritarian rule and limited and non-accountable political pluralism. There is no elaborate ideology to guide it like totalitarianism, but there are different mentalities, which rather defend and justify the existing political structure underpinned by customs and tradition. These regimes are characterized as a whole that solves public problems without asking the people. In this way, this group seeks the demobilization of members of civil society by encouraging political apathy, to the extent that it is not contrary to their interests. In most cases these regimes are radically transitory as they depend on a founding charismatic leader, missing the leader can proceed to a democratic or totalitarian regime.

b) Democratic regimes: Democratic regimes are characterized by the division of political power into different bodies. The authorities are elected in free, competitive and transparent elections, the political task of the opposition is accepted and encouraged, there is a respect and guarantee for the rights of the people and in general the titles, principles and attributes of freedom prevail. The political system of Chile established by the current constitution establishes that we are a republican, democratic and representative political system, with a presidential or presidential type government, it is a form of government in which the States divided into three independent powers such as executive, legislative and judicial.

At the head of the government is the executive branch, the president of the republic, who is elected by popular and direct suffrage by all citizens entitled to vote (over 18 years of age and who do not serve distressing sentences), for periods of four years and without the right to immediate re-election.

Legislative power resides in the national congress, which is located in the city of Valparaiso in region V. The congress has the powers of overseer and co-legislator, which is also bicameral with two chambers such as: senators with 38 members and deputies with 120 members.

The judiciary is an independent and autonomous part of the government which is responsible for the administration of justice. The highest court of this power is the Supreme Court, composed of 21 members, one of whom is elected by the president every three years.

With all the above, we begin to draw the first traces of the institutional system that allows us to live together and make decisions.

Chile is a democracy, a state of law, we have a market economy. The values of our model of harmony are support, political pluralism and respect for fundamental rights and public freedoms.

The fundamental charter best known as a constitution protects the rights of individuals and establishes principles to guide the actions of the public authorities.

Some features of this constitutional framework stand out:

a) Right to equality, non-discrimination, freedom of ideology, religion, expression, assembly, demonstration, association, political parties, trade unions and strike.
b) Private property.
c) Promote public participation through representatives and in some cases directly.
d) Pay attention to education, health, social. Reference is made to work and housing. Considering consumers, families. Assessment of science, culture, heritage and the environment.

e) Rights are complemented by duties for all, respect the law, the rights of others.

f) Sovereignty belongs to the Chilean Government and consequently to the people, that is to say, to all Chileans, from it derives the powers of the State: executive, legislative, judicial.

g) It establishes the unity of the State and the autonomy of the regions

h) Common institutions for all

i) 16 autonomous regions.

Like other States, Chile has grown in economic and international political skills.

CHAPTER 14

Foreign policy and economic relations

Chile's foreign policy is set by the president of the republic, who has the objective of principles of international action and Chile interests in the world.

These elements make possible the policies, guidelines and concrete actions, whose implementation falls under the responsibility of the Ministry of Foreign Affairs.

Chile's development depends fundamentally on foreign trade and foreign policy. As time passes, our international relations become stronger, which is a means of promoting the internationalization of our economy, strengthening trade promotion and fostering national economic and social development.

The objective of foreign policy is to seek ways to project ourselves to the main commercial markets of the world and to promote both the diversification and growth of our exports through the negotiation, implementation and administration of trade agreements, the development and promotion of exports of goods and services, in order to attract investment, and Chile's participation in international economic forums and organizations.

The principles of Chilean foreign policy are the main fundamental guidelines that underpin and relate to the decisions taken by Chile in foreign relations cases. They are the orientations of higher hierarchy that guide our external management.

1) International law: there are several fundamental norms that define and structure the international legal order, and promote peaceful bilateral relations between the various States, Chile attaches special importance to the following rights:

a) validity of treaties: International stability and the peaceful coexistence of States are indispensable conditions for the development of nations. Respect for the commitments made is, in this respect, an essential principle of our society. That is why, at the global level, Chile attaches fundamental value to treaties as a necessary source for promoting peaceful international relations, legal security and cooperation among States through clear and stable rules.

b) Peaceful solutions to disputes: Through this principle we reiterate our attachment to the prohibition of the threat or use of force in international relations that is contrary to the principles established in the Charter of the United Nations, as well as our conviction that diplomacy and law are the only legitimate means for the settlement of international disputes. Chile, as a pioneering member of the United Nations (UN), attaches essential value to the strict application of its principles, supporting all initiatives aimed at achieving peaceful solutions to international conflicts.

c) Independence and respect for sovereignty: Chile attaches particular importance to the principle of the sovereign equality of States as an essential norm for the respect and peaceful coexistence of international society. That is why our nation is opposed to the intervention of one or more nations in the internal affairs of another nation and believes that only international law can establish demands and limitations on them. The political and economic self-determination of States and geographical integrity are fundamental values in this regard. While recognizing the evolution of international law in areas such as human rights, we share the view that humanitarian actions for qualified cases, authorized in the multilateral framework of the United Nations, can be used in serious situations of risk to the population.

d) Territorial integrity: The preservation of the integrity of its territory and its political independence is fundamental for Chile and is ensured through diplomacy and the tools offered by international law. The characteristic of Chilean space, which includes maritime, air and Chilean Antarctic Territory, entails important demands and responsibilities for our country.

2) Democracy and respect for human rights: Democracy is the political system that constitutes the appropriate framework for full respect for the essential rights of every human being. The values of tolerance, dialogue, equal opportunities, social inclusion and cohesion, as well as the full exercise of fundamental freedoms, are best guaranteed in a context where the rule of law prevails and where public policies act effectively. Chile appreciates that the rights of

individuals, as an inalienable attribute of every human being, should be observed in all circumstances, times and places.

Hence our adherence to international instruments and mechanisms for the protection of human rights, which must be complementary to national systems and exercised when local means do not exist or, if they exist, are not effective.

.

3) Responsibility to cooperate: State and non-state actors interact in international life with an intensity hitherto unknown. This table creates important opportunities for collaboration among States and theirs with other international actors to face new international challenges and threats together and with increasingly effective tools. Thus, climate change, epidemics, food security, environmental degradation, ethnic conflicts, humanitarian difficulties, transnational organized crime, human trafficking, among others, require joint action. A broad-based cooperative approach is essential in addressing global risks. Chile is therefore firmly committed to cooperating, through its technical and human resources, in all multilateral, universal, regional, subregional and bilateral forums, in order to cooperate in solving these problems.

Foreign economy, Chile prides itself on having an open and stable economic model that favors trade and investment, which is respected and praised in the world.

In the last ten years it has developed a progressive network of trade agreements with Bolivia, Brunei, Canada, Central America, China, Colombia, South Korea, Cuba, Ecuador, the United States, India, Iceland, Liechtenstein, MERCOSUR, Mexico, Norway, New Zealand, Panama, Peru, Singapore, Switzerland, the European Union and Venezuela.

Jointly, in March 2007, Chile signed a Free Trade Agreement with Japan. More than 76% of Chilean shipments go to these markets, which account for 87% of global GDP.

The free trade agreements together with the trade agreements signed with most Latin American countries, allow Chile privileged access to a market of 3,800 million inhabitants in the world, which makes the country an original bridge between Latin America and Asia Pacific.

CHAPTER 15

Comparative politics

Comparative politics is a sub branch of political science, characterized by an approach based on the comparative method.

Comparative policy is a methodology focused on the how, but does not specify the what of the analysis. Comparative politics is not defined by the objective it studies, but rather by the method it applies to the study of political phenomena, when these are applied to specific fields of policy studies.

Comparative politics may be known by other names, such as comparative government which is the comparative study of forms of government, or foreign policy of different states to establish general empirical connections between the characteristics of the state and the characteristics of its foreign policy.

The comparative method is an empiric, statistical and case study method. The present method is one of the fundamental scientific methods that can be used to test general empirical validity, that is, to establish empirical relationships between two or more variables while the other variables remain constant overtime.

The comparative method is generally used when neither the experimental nor the statistical method can be used, in certain very rare occasions or extraordinarily experiments are conducted in political science, on the other hand, the statistical method involves mathematical manipulation in quantitative cases over a large number of case numbers, while political research has to be analyzed or seen qualitatively in the numbers of cases collected.

The approximation of case studies cannot be used or considered a scientific method according to the above statement, however, it can be used to gain information on singular cases, the same ones that can be used in comparison according to the comparative method.

Comparative strategies, there are several strategies, all different which can be used in comparative research.

A) The thousand similarity method: such a method consists of comparing several similar cases, which differ only in the dependent variable, in theory assuming that this will make it easier to find those independent variables that can be explained in the presence or absence of the dependent variable.

B) The method of the difference of a thousand: similar to the previous method consists of comparing several different cases, all of which have in common the same dependent variable, so that any other circumstance that is present in all cases can be considered as the independent variable.

CHAPTER 16

Economics in politics

The expression political economy was first introduced by the French economist Antoine de Month resting in 1615, who used this term to refer to the study of production relations, especially between the main classes of bourgeois society or proletariat. The theory of physiocracy, in which it is postulated that the earth was the origin of all wealth.

Adam Smith recognized economist and one of the greatest exponents of classical economics, within the term political economy proposed the theory of the value of labor, according to which labor is the real source of value. Which was disproved by Carl Manger in establishing the theory of subject value.

Towards the end of the nineteenth century, political economy was abandoned by the general term economics, used by those who sought to abandon the classist view of society, replacing it with the mathematical approach, current economic studies, and who conceive the value originated in the utility that the good generated by the individual.

Today, the term political economy is still used to refer to interdisciplinary studies that rely on economics, sociology, anthropology, law and political science which use the term to understand how institutions and political environments influence the conduct of markets.

Within political science, economics refers mainly to liberal, Marxist or other theories that study the relations of economics and political power within the State.

International political economy I seen change, a branch of economics that concerns foreign trade, international finance and government policies that affect international trade between nations, such as monetary and fiscal policies.

Political economy studies the relationships that individuals establish with each other to organize collective production, especially those relationships that are established between the owners of the means of production and the workers.

The economy of subjective value focuses on prices and sees the production and consumption of people as effects of these, on the other hand, political economy sees economic activity as the result of the survival needs of the human being, conformed in a community and its legal, technoscientific and cultural determinations.

The division between the value of use and value of exchange, which is made distension clearly established by Karl Mark in capital, in which it establishes a separation between what is now known as value and price, from the perspective of the total identification of value with price in schools of subjective value.

Private exchange occurs in the market and is based on a legal framework that validates private property. This sector is called the private sector.

When the government intervenes in the market economy, through policies or direct exchanges, it is called the public sector.

The physiocrats considered that the only economic activity is the production of agricultural or raw materials.

The United States is the world's largest economy, ahead of China. After a decade of growth, GDP growth was negative in 2020 (-4.3%, IMF) following the COVID-19 crisis, deepened by growing inequalities and outdated infrastructure, which are slowing potential GDP growth. Despite the signing of a partial trade deal in January 2020, trade tensions persist with China; most tariffs remain in place (19% on average in early 2020, compared to 3% in early 2018). From what can be foreseen from the program of the new president-elect Joe Biden, trade threats against Europe should disappear, while trade tensions with China should be lowered. After a deep contraction in the second quarter of 2020, which reflected the impact of containment measures, the U.S. economy rebounded strongly with an annualized rate of 33.1%, although the second wave of infections generated new restrictions, making the situation even more uncertain. According to the IMF's October 2020 forecasts, GDP growth should pick up to 3.1% this year, stabilizing at around 2.9% in 2022, assuming the global crisis subsides thanks to different vaccines against COVID-19. In the most recent update of its World Economic Outlook, the IMF revised its growth projections for the United States, indicating 5.1% in 2021 and 2.5% in 2022 (corresponding to a difference of +2% and -0.4% respectively from the WTO's October 2020 projection). In 2020, the budget deficit reached a record level of 15% as a result of measures taken to mitigate the impact of the COVID-19 crisis (around 14% of GDP). This budget deficit should be progressively reduced in 2021 and 2022 (to 7.6% and 6.1% respectively, IMF). The ratio of government debt to GDP, which is already on an upward trend in recent years, increased considerably during 2020 to finance spending to support households and businesses, reaching 131.2%. This trend is expected to continue, bringing the deficit to 134.5% of GDP in 2022. The United States, however, enjoys unparalleled financial flexibility as the issuer of the U.S. dollar, the largest reserve currency in the world. President-elect Joe Biden's multibillion-dollar stimulus plan could lead to a $5.4 trillion spending increase over the next decade in areas such as infrastructure, clean energy, manufacturing, education and health, while taxes on high-income and corporate should increase by $3.4 trillion over 10 years. According to the IMF, the inflation rate fell by 1.5% in 2020 (compared to 1.8% a year earlier, due to pressure on household incomes and low energy prices), below the Fed's 2% target. However, inflation is expected to jump to 2.8% in 2021, before falling back to 2.1% the following year, although this depends largely on lab our market performance. The impact of the COVID-19 crisis was particularly harsh on the U.S. labor market. According to the December 2020 Employment Situation described by the Bureau of Labor Statistics, in November the unemployment rate tilted to 6.7%; this rate is down 8% from its recent highest figure in April, but is 3.2% higher than in February. The number of unemployed people, at 10.7 million, continued to fall in November, but is still 4.9 million higher than in February. The IMF forecasts an unemployment rate of 7.3% in 2021, which will fall again in 2022 to 5.7%. U.S. citizens enjoy one of the highest GDP per capita in the world, estimated at $65,118 in 2019 by the World Bank. However, current public health policies tend to worsen inequalities: The number of people without insurance increased during the Trump administration. In 2019, there were 34 million people in poverty, approximately 4.2 million fewer than in 2018 (U.S. Census). According to a Columbia University study, however, the monthly poverty rate increased from 15% to 16.7% from February to September 2020 due to the crisis generated by the COVID-19 pandemic.

The United States is a highly industrialized country with high levels of productivity and use of modern technologies. Key sectors include agriculture (maize, soybeans, beef and cotton); machinery manufacturing, chemicals, food and automobiles and booming tertiary market focused on finance, insurance, real estate, leases and leases. The American Agricultural sector is undoubtedly one of the largest in the world, and California itself produces more than one-third of the country's vegetables and two-thirds of its fruits and nuts. However, agriculture only accounts for 0.9% of GDP and employs 1% of the workforce (World Bank, 2019). According to data from the U.S. Department of Agriculture, also considering the food and related industries, the primary sector contributed USD 1.109 trillion to the country's GDP in 2019, with a share of 5.2% (the results of U.S. farms alone represent 136,100 million USD). In the same year, 22.2 million full-time or part-time jobs were related to the agriculture and food sectors. The Department of Agriculture expects net agricultural income to increase by USD 18,300 million (21.7%) in 2019 to 102,700 million in 2020, despite the COVID-19 crisis. In fact, while actual agricultural product revenues are expected to fall by USD 15,200 million (4.1%), direct government agricultural payments should increase by 64.4% (to USD 14,600 million). Including a wide range of activities, the industrial sector contributes about 18.2% of GDP and employs 20% of the workforce. In addition to the industries mentioned above, the country is also a world leader in the aerospace and pharmaceutical industries. Thanks to its abundant natural resources, the United States has become a leader in the production of a quantity of minerals, and has been able to maintain a diversified production. The country is the largest producer of natural liquid gas, aluminum, electricity and nuclear power. It is also the world's third largest producer of oil and, for years, has also been developing large-scale shale gas extraction. According to the latest figures from the Bureau of Economic Analysis, industries producing private goods fell by 34.4% in the second quarter of 2020, following the COVID-19 pandemic. This huge drop largely reflects a decline in the manufacture of durable goods (led by motor vehicles, bodies and caravans, and parts). The U.S. economy is essentially service-based. The tertiary sector contributes more than three quarters of GDP (77.4%) and employs more than 79% of the country's workforce. A large part of GDP is made up of the finance, insurance, real estate, rent and leasing sectors (21% in 2019); as well as professional and commercial services (12.8%). The government sector (at the federal, state, and local levels) contributed about 12.3% of the country's GDP in 2019 (U.S. Department of Commerce). The Bureau of Economic Analysis estimates that the decline in private service producing industries in the second quarter of 2020 was mainly due to the decline in lodging and food services activities (which represented -4.38% change in real GDP); health care and social assistance (4.38% change in real GDP, especially outpatient health care); and transport and storage (-2.56% of GDP, and the air transport sector was the hardest hit).

CHAPTER 17

administration

The administration can be defined with the following quote "the coordinated effort of a social group to obtain an end with the greatest efficiency and the least possible effort" (Münch Galindo & García Martínez, 1990), this quote means that a group of people can balance a series of activities through an administrative process in order to reach a common end.

There are a series of rules that must be followed in the administration such as: plan which must design an action plan for the future, organization its function is to provide and mobilize the resources available to implement our plan, direct is select and evaluate employees in order to achieve the best work to achieve what was planned , coordinating is the integration of efforts and ensuring that information is shared and problems are solved, controlling is ensuring that things happen according to plan and execution of the necessary corrective actions of the deviations found.

Administration is an essential task in a pluralistic society that is based on the effort of the person through organizations, The basic task of administration is to do things through people, with the best results, in any example of human organization efficiency and effectiveness is sought.

Administration is the set of solutions that allows citizens and companies to interact with the public administration through electronic means.

It could be assimilated to the creation of a virtual window, a single window that allows the provision of public services by administrators to citizens and businesses.

People, by interacting with the administration through these electronic means, will perceive greater transparency and control over the procedure of any procedure by the initiated. You will certainly notice a substantial improvement in the clarity of the service provided by the administration.

For the administration, this new form of relationship and provision of services, which involve publishing electronically the information of interest to the citizenry and facilitating the electronic transmission of the acts of the administration that people do in person.

It should be noted that the development of this new mode of relationship with the administration does not replace the current one in which people carry out various face-to-face procedures, it is, therefore, the decision of each person to choose the mode of relationship with the administration.

Today we find ourselves in a context of modernization of the services provided to society, in which citizens and companies demand the need for a new model of relationship with public administration.

Therefore, the public administration must adapt to the context in order to be able to provide the services demanded by people and people in general. In this area of eGovernment, the main factors influencing and encouraging modernization initiatives are:

- The evolution of new right of persons and duties by parts of persons and duties by parts of public administration.
- Changes in the approaches to action of the public administration.
- Socio-economic changes.
- New possibilities of information and communication technologies in the field of public management.

The advantages of the new eGovernment are manifold and offer benefits both for citizens and for companies, as well as for the administration itself.

They are as follows:

a) Availability: interact and carry out administrative procedures 24 hours a day. It is not necessary to adapt to an office schedule.

b) Ease of access: which will no longer allow it to be necessary to go to the offices in person to carry out the procedures, can be done from anywhere in the world through the telephone or internet.

c) Time saving: to be able to manage it can be done from home or anywhere we want, without the need to travel to an office in person.

d) Simplification of the procedures: as for the applicant they will not need to present documents that the administration already has due to previous procedures.

The main advantage that public administration has is the simplification of administrative procedures.

-   Reduction of some costs and processing times.

-   Increase in transactions made by people.

-   Reduction of the papers and files necessary for processing.

-   Improved transaction security.

-   Eliminations of the need to enter the same information in
    several systems.

CHAPTER 18

Leadership and management

In the various organizations that exist the organization is concentrated through its collaborators, in other words, its human team, a lot of talent. Or at least, this should be one of the main objectives at a strategic level, to attract and retain the best talent in order to offer the market excellence in services.

In this sense we can distinguish different types of talents, all of them important for their contribution in the teamwork that makes both the company or the public administration. If we start with the largest base of the leadership of work organizations, as a general rule, we will find the individual collaborators.

Individual collaborators are those roles in which individual responsibility and people are responsible for their own work. Then we will find the next group, smaller in size that are the middle managers, here this type of people has responsibility for their own team, but also for the contribution that their team makes to the organization.

Then we find the executives who are the ones who direct these middle managers and finally in the highest positions and responsibility we find the people who occupy management, senior management or presidency roles.

The above description is a generalization how talent is structured within organizations although it is true that each organization has its peculiar systems and can be structured differently. But what it's all about is understanding with this structure is the idea that leadership and managerial skills are needed in most employees.

The importance of leadership depends and will depend on the position the person is using within the organization.

The main managerial skills can be classified into different groups, technical, human and conceptual skills. Within these three categories, we could define the following.

- Self-knowledge and self-financing: the primary step to be a good manager and be able to improve is to know ourselves, to know our strengths and weaknesses, we can know each other more with the realization of a SWOT or SWOT which will help us to know our strengths, opportunities, weaknesses and threats. Which would be useful for us to know our leadership style and how we relate to others.
- Vision and strategic thinking: all employees and especially those in a position of responsibility must be able to participate and make decisions in line with strategy.
- Information management and business knowledge: it deals with all the external information systems of the market and have the ability to analyze it, decide what information is relevant to each situation, transfer it to your team so that they are informed and that all this helps you to make a good decision.
- Communication: it is essential that managers have excellent skills in terms of communication management, both at the level of information management as we have just mentioned, and communication is one of the keys to team management.

- Negotiation capacity, crisis management and changes: having the tools and experience to negotiate with different stakeholders. This also involves the management of complicated situations in which internal or external crises occur, or situations involving structural changes within the organization.

- Project management: it is not enough to develop a strategy, but then this must be transferred to the day to day and therefore perform the implementation. To do this, the people who occupy these positions with more responsibility and who have teams in their charge will have to be able to successfully direct and manage the projects that are within their areas.

- Control and management of talent: it will be essential to carry out a control of the employees, but also thinking that it is addressing people and that the focus is to manage the talent that is within an organization so that it not only stays in administrative control, but that we are able to help those people evolve, grow within a public or private company and that it develops talent back to the system that may exist in the company.

International intelligence and emotional skills and social skills are very important for leadership.

Leadership is an essential skill, without leadership everything else is meaningless, leadership style is a common thread that will make the rest of the skills can develop and come together to motivate and lead teams.

CHAPTER 19

Ethics and Governance

When there is no state or a global government, international relations are safeguarded by multiple institutions of global governments, including treaty-based organizations, as well as various formal and informal bodies in global society. But what ethical limitations apply to it? The present actors that make up the bodies of global governments are State, which are subject to strict ethical limitations because they play major roles in global practices, the society of sovereign states. It has values that restrict them from such practices such as freedom and diversity. Since individuals make up the institutions of global government, they are required to promote both ethical values.

At present there is no world state, therefore a global government. Instead, today's contemporary world consists of 194 sovereign States coexisting in a globalized world order. Which coexist in a world with transnational interactions that over time have led to the creation of international organizations of one kind or another. These include churches, multinational companies, scientific organizations, sports bodies, to name but a few.

There is an immensity of literature, on the process of globalization, within this world has emerged a need for transnational rules of conduct to guide those immersed in this global interaction. Transnational rules are required for coordination, conflict prevention, dispute resolution, standardization, among other matters.

Nowhere is this more evident than the field of international banking, given that it is faced with the global financial crisis. Without such social regulatory rules in current globalized international practices.

There is a series of functional rules which is a prerequisite for the ongoing development of our international order, the rules must be effective and binding for the participation of society in globalization.

The creation of a regulated global order requires global governance institutions capable of creating regulatory frameworks that can link all actors in a functional and specific field.

This leaves the following question or intrigue, what are the institutions of global governance that offer rules, in the absence of a global state or consequently a government?

Answering the previous question that in closes the previous paragraph. There are many and diverse organizations that have addressed the elaboration of rules for a globalized world, putting the establishment of the appropriate regulatory practices, from those treated as, the UN, NATO or the IMF, to a large number of different types of governmental organizations (NGOs) a detailed classification of such organizations could well be the subject of an entire treaty.

Despite the variety of mechanism for a global government, it is relevant to point out certain general characteristics about agreements of governments established in this world that lacks a global government. Firstly, all these bodies will be limited to specific areas of competence, drawing up rules relating to specific functions and activities such as banking, the environment or energy production and distribution.

The jurisdictions of the global governance body are limited to particular functions and often to specific geographical areas. Secondly, many government agencies overlap in their scope of action. Thirdly, none of them possesses the sovereignty which primarily characterizes the State; fourthly, these organizations see the light of day at different times with different objectives. And finally, as a fifth element, the network of government bodies is constantly flowing.

This implies the entry that there are often clashes concerning who is competent to lay down rules, about what and in what areas.

Institutions of government are not born out of a vacuum, but are created within existing global practices by actors involved in those same practices. The two key practices that are cultivated by international government institutions are two anarchic practices. On the one hand, we have sovereign societies, and on the other hand global society. Both are strict sense which means that it is the need to observe voluntarily a behavior, in favor of the general community or a certain person.

It must be understood that in both cases the individual actors formed by practice have equal freedoms and are not subject to any sovereign government. Sovereign States are the central actors, men and women are regarded as holders of rights. These actors make it up the practice.

The creation of a world order requires and needs global governmental institutions.

Looking at the existence of a wide range of bodies involved in global governance, a fundamental question arises: are these bodies ethical? Although it sounds common to ask this question about our formal state structures, as we often do is to make ethical judgments about absolutist monarchical characteristics, totalitarian states, authoritarian states or failed and weak states.

It is less common to raise it in relation to the bodies in charge of the global bodies. In making ethical judgments about sovereign states, let us appeal to democratic theory, human rights theory, as well as justice theory, among others. There are debates, essays on the benefits of social democracies in the face of the evils of totalitarian e-state. More complex are the discussions, often in embroidery, about the ethical pros and cons of different types of democracies.

Similarly, there are complex and heated debates about different types of electoral systems. In the international arena it is always discussed, often ethically argued about the advantages and disadvantages of the society of sovereign states in comparison with some other imaginable international order such as the Communist one. Likewise, ethical debates are created in axes to our contemporary systems for the universal distribution of scarce resources and about the freedom, or lack thereof, of people to move around the planet to their liking. These debates are fuel led by theories of international justice.

Government bodies are many and very diverse, and because they are less well understood than sovereign states. In order to calm this unethical global governance.

The starting point is to emphasize that many of the different government structures in world politics are the work of actors immersed in the two practices briefly mentioned above. Those who establish government institutions are one of two, or sovereign states in society, or individual men and women who have rights in global society. Such actors do not exist in nothing, but are constituted as what they are within global governance.

An important implication is that these characters are constrained by the ethical values involved in the practices in which they themselves have constituted themselves as e-states or as individual right holders. The fact of a social constitution inflicts ethical limitations on what institutions of government it would be appropriate to create on its part.

There is a whole succession of areas in global business within which the actors today seek   to raise appropriate government structures. There are areas where government is urgent at the moment: finance, banking, global warming, food distribution, global terrorism, international migration and the regulation of private military companies. These are just some of the many issues.

The actors seeking to engage with them are both individuals and individuals who often work through specific partnerships, as has now been pointed out, these actors are not free, waiting for some limbo to create appropriate global government structures. Furthermore, they are not properly considered free actors to choose which code of ethics to apply in their appropriate forms of governments that are required to be introduced, to such actors who are already highly sophisticated global pieces in which there are integrated elaborate codes of ethics.

The sovereign States. It is to be constituted as such in the practices of the sovereign States, by which I mean that it consists of being a participating State is determined by other States within the practices of the States. For any recognition by the rest of the E state as a legitimate participant, it is essential to be a complete participant.

There are many entities in the world that wish to become participants in the society of states. However, they have not yet received recognition. The recognition requirement mentioned here is common to the set of social practices. Football club, church, schools, universities, private clubs, etc.

They have internal rules and regulations on the prior criteria that must be applied for an actor to be recognized, one of the key characteristics to become a participant in a social practice is that the actor in question must understand, accept and promote ethical values. For example, students must accept the ethical commitments that this institution establishes in its manual of coexistence, which includes, among other things, committing to the search for the truth of knowledge, submitting to the right of evidence and rejecting traps. Similarly, entities that are accepted into the practice of e-state must accept the values associated with this practice. These are a commitment to the sovereign autonomy of individual States and an acceptance of the values of diversity between States within practice, accepting that some States will be socialist, some liberal, some communist, others Islamic, etc. In such a society the participants have the right to be different from each other.

To give an example, sovereign States have gained the possibility of forging certain alliances or agreements with other States, the freedom that makes it possible to carry out internal policies such as those decided by their own citizens, as well as being able to consider and implement their own diplomatic and economic agreements at international level.

The States must learn the consequences of launching attacks or military aggressions against other sovereign States, the consequence being the illegality of trying to impose their policies on other States, in breach of international contracts. Participants must understand and understand that actions would be unethical.

The second major global practice is the building of units for global governance. To understand that global society is a global practice that includes as a participant anyone anywhere. In global society, people constitute each other, through a process of mutual recognition, as holders of human rights. Freedoms are recognized, including the right to personal integrity, the right of movement, freedom of association, freedom of conscience, as well as the right to private property.

The core elements linked to the defining rights of practice as a whole are the values of individual autonomy and the value of diversity. It is not possible to make sense of rights without assuming that participants value the freedom and diversity that their freedom in turn   makes possible.

Rights holders can use their right in different ways. Rights create and nurture various outlets, within the global society, as well as the society of the States, there are certain requirements that must be met, the main thing is to respect the rights of others. The second thing is for people to feed the diversity that arises through the rights of others.

Rights guarantee a person with a series of actions, most of which allows different types of association of rights. Basically, you are required not to abuse the rights of others. In the final instance, the abuse of the rights of others could lead to abuse by the rest of the right holders.

It is crucial for this chapter to understand that all those responsible for creating government structures in order to be able to deal with the above issues participate simultaneously in daily practices, and are therefore bound by ethical values. At the same time, there are so many players within the society of sovereign states, as citizens in global society as right holders.

All people, everywhere and at all times have the same inalienable universal rights, as well as a numberless number of other local practices such as family, church, school, private clubs, etc. With the passage of time, it takes changes to adapt to the new times. It is often the case that what is ethically required of one practice may conflict with what is ethically required in another.

Finding ways to resolve these tensions is critical to government-linked planning and policy-making. For example, if there were inherent internment between what is ethically demanded in global society such as the claim to and respect for individual human rights, and what is ethically required of a person in the society of sovereign states, and the protection of his or her autonomy.

In some cases, it may seem that doing the latter requires ignoring government issues linked to migrants. Faced with such issues, people must look for ways to resolve such tensions, if they do not want their lives to be affected by ethical contradictions. One way of doing this would be to insist that the States and their governments, in all their actions, also promote the rights of the global society of free individuals.

CHAPTER 20

History of constitutions

To start with history, you have to start with the following question Why are constitutions created? The first thing to understand what a constitution is, we have to know why constitutions were created, and how they have evolved over time. This is important to understand that it is a constitution.

a) the constitution does not come out of nowhere

b) Chile has a constitution tradition

(c) the types of constitution that exist

Constitutionalism: constitutionalism arises in England during the seventeenth century as a reaction or solution to absolutism. Absolutism promoted the idea that kings could concentrate all power in their hands, without being bound by law.

Din he rent right that the State must respect: constitutionalism claimed the old ideas that no one can be above the law, that no one can be above the law, that no one can claim to monopolize the law, and that all people have certain inherent rights which the State must respect.

Constitution in the world: Constitutionalism and its ideas took root in the 13 North American colonies (USA) of England, giving the origin later to a promising nation that is the United States of America and to the first written constitution in the world and which would be the example of many others.

Documents of nominee (constitution): although from the nineteenth century in the countries of the West specifically in the American continent arise these new documents of nominee's "constitutions", these new documents often dealt well with the organization of power. But they lacked the constitutional spirit, i.e., the idea of limiting power.

Rights, freedoms and limitation of power: that remains more or less the same over time, until after the Second World War, when the defense of rights, freedoms and the limitation of power became the main or rather the center of the constitutional text which emerged from that period.

CHILE in its first 100 years: Chile, in its beginnings (in its first years) as a nation, had a series of constitutional texts (8 between 1810 and 1833) that try to create a certain institutional in the country. Although it cannot be consolidated, these texts begin to outline some aspects that will remain in the organization of the Republic: a president in charge of the government, a congress with two chambers, and a division between the powers of the State.

1833 first lasting constitution: In 1833 the first lasting constitution is issued. With it, the foundations of the Chilean constitutional tradition begin to be consolidated, such as presidentialism, some rights, and the powers of congress.

Constitution of 1925 reaffirms the presidentialism: the constitution of 1925 as it says in its title reaffirms the so-called presidentialism, ensures a more complete list of rights and freedoms and creates institutions such as the qualifying court of elections and in one of its modifications, the constitutional court.

1980 continues the presidential system: The constitution of 1980 continues the presidential system, a bicameral congress, regulates again the qualifying court of elections and the constitutional court, and incorporates the regulation of the comptroller general of the republic and the central bank. But its main novelty is the incorporation of a special remedy to give effect to the protection of rights and freedoms recognized in the constitution the remedy of protection.

Restrictions on public freedoms: however, this constitution was drafted during a dictatorial government (military dictatorship) in simple words during a government not democratically elected. The plebiscite ratified took place when there was no electoral register in Chile and the country was in a state of siege, that is to say, there were restrictions on public freedoms.

Principals' reforms: multiple articles of the constitution have been reformed through its almost 40 years of validity. The main reforms were those of 1989 and 2005, which were achieved thanks to the agreements of various political sectors.

1989 reform: the 1989 reform strengthened the protection of fundamental rights and greater civic participation.

Reform of 2005: the reform of 2005 was of such magnitude, that when it was promulgated, it was presented as a new constitution, symbol of which is the signature of President Ricardo Lagos. Some of the amendments included were the elimination of appointed senators, the increase of control functions of the chamber of deputies, and the increase of the powers of the constitutional court.

What is the constitution for today? To answer this question, it is necessary to know what are the minimum contents of a constitution to achieve its end.

Have we read our own constitution in detail? Do we know its purpose and why it is so important? Like the recognized historical antecedents, the constitution is a limit to power through law, in order to sensors and safeguard the fundamental rights and freedoms of individuals.

Answering the question, what is the constitution for today?

It is not a simple set of rules designed to organize the powers orthostates.

It is not an instrument at the service of power, but of the people

It has limits, because a constitution that does not limit power or recognize fundamental rights is not truly a constitution.

To achieve limitation to power, there are certain limited contents that have to be in a constitution.

1. Recognition of the rule of law or rule of law

The rule of law or the rule of law is a procedure designed to curb power through the law. The law is above the government and the authorities. The law delimits the powers of state organs.

This principle of the rule of law has been recognized in the Chilean Constitutions of 1833, 1925 and 1980.

UDS will wonder how the limitation of authorities, the same authorities that make laws and regulations, will be achieved.

This will be achieved through the supremacy of the constitution. But this means, it means that the constitution is above power, specifying the powers of the authorities, the constitution is above all other rules governing a country. It has a higher hierarchy than laws, regulations and any other rule issued by an authority of any kind. No rule, laws or regulations can go against what the constitution says, the constitution is above the bodies that produce such rules. Thebes' example of this is congress or the president.

Consequences of constitutional supremacy to protect the supremacy of the constitution, there are generally more stringent requirements for amending the constitution than for changing the law.

today most laws in Chile are approved by the majority of parliamentarians present. On the other hand, in order to approve an amendment to the Constitution, 3/5 of the deputies and senators in office are required as a general rule, and for some matters 2/3 of the parliamentarians in office. In other Latin American countries, the 2/3 reinforced majority approval system is also used, which is what happens in Ecuador, Uruguay and Argentina, for example. Likewise, constitutional systems protect constitutional supremacy with other mechanisms, such as the approval of parliament by a special quorum, and also a referendum or plebiscite (Spanish Constitution, for example), or the approval by an absolute majority of the chambers, but with two successive votes, mediating between each vote a certain period (Italian Constitution, for example), among other ways.

The idea is that the legislator cannot change the content of the Constitution through a law.

To ensure the supremacy of the Constitution, there must be institutions and mechanisms to ensure that Congress and the president do not issue rules contrary to the Constitution. In ours, these bodies are the Constitutional Court, the Office of the Comptroller General of the Republic and the Courts of Justice. The essential role of the Constitutional Court is to monitor the constitutionality of laws. In Chile it was introduced into our legal system by the constitutional reform of 1970 to the Constitution of 1925, although it exists in many countries (Germany, France, Spain, Italy, Colombia, etc.). In countries where there is no Constitutional Court, courts of law have to check that the law does not contradict the Constitution (e.g., United States, Argentina, Brazil).

But it more needs to be regulated in a constitution to have detailed some basic definitions of organization which, in the end, relate to the division of powers.

It should also contain a mechanism to reform it. If this is not provided for, the constitutions become obsolete and there is no choice but a new constitution.

CHAPTER 21

Frequently asked questions from people

As citizens we have different questions about the current situation that we are living as a people and as a nation.

How many constitutions has Chile had?

Chile has had 10 constitutions: 1811, 1812, 1814, 1818, 1822, 1823, 1828, 1833, 1925 and 1980.

What should a constitution have?

It must contain the system of separation of powers, designing its structure, assigning the powers and competences to each power of the State, as well as the list of the rights and freedoms which are accorded to individuals and the mechanisms which enable them to be guaranteed.

What is democracy?

Democracy is the form of government in which power is exercised by the authorities elected by the people in periodic, free, secret and informed elections.

What is the rule of law?

It is an essential principle of constitutionalism, which requires the submission of state power to the Constitution, to laws, to judicial rulings, to the dignity and essential rights of the human being.

What is the separation of powers?

It is an essential principle of constitutionalism, which is that the various functions of State power are exercised by various organs: legislative, executive and judicial.

What rights should be included in a constitution?

If we look at the origins of constitutionalism, we can see that it was born with the purpose of defending and protecting at least the following rights, which should be recognized and protected by any constitution: the right to due process (presumption of innocence, right to defense, right to impartiality of the judge, etc.); equality before the law (preventing arbitrary, unreasonable privileges); the right to life (right not to be unjustly deprived of life and the right to defend it); the right to property (right not to be arbitrarily deprived of property); freedom of association (right to establish associations); freedom of religion and conscience (the right to profess or not to profess a faith, to manifest it publicly, and not to be forced to go against the conscience); the right to vote and to stand as a candidate (to elect and to be elected). The peculiarity of these rights lies in the fact that, from the legal point of view, in the event of violation or threat of violation, they can be protected and protected by the judges simply because they are recognized in the Constitution.

What are social rights?

Social rights are a manifestation of the legitimate aspiration for social justice on the part of a political community. As a general rule, they constitute principles and program of social policy, which must be developed and implemented by the legislative and executive branches, in accordance with the country's economic resources. Based on their development and legislative implementation, they could be protected and protected by judges.

In either of the two scenarios above, would it be possible to amend the current Constitution?

Yes, applying the reform procedure of Chapter XV.

How can the current Constitution be amended?

Under Chapter XV of the Constitution, the power of reform rests with the National Congress. The legislative initiative to propose a reform belongs both to the president of the Republic and to any of the deputies or senators. The general rule is that to reform the Constitution requires in each chamber of 3/5 of the deputies and senators in office. But to change Chapters I (Bases of Institutionalist), III (constitutional rights and duties), VIII

(Constitutional Court), XI (Armed Forces, Order and Public Security), XII (National Security Council) or XV (Reform of the Constitution), you will need, in each Chamber, the approval of the 2/3 of the deputies and senators in office.

Why is it said that the current Constitution provides for a subsidiary state?

Because according to Article 1 of the current Constitution, the State recognizes, protects and guarantees the adequate autonomy of civil society, that is, of what this article calls "intermediate groups through which society is organized and structured". Subsidiarity has two meanings. The first implies that the State must come to the aid ("subsidies") of the smaller communities and of the people in need. An example of this is the economic measures taken by the State to help people who have lost their jobs and income due to the health contingency caused by Covid-19 (bonds, loans, food). The second implies that the State does not interfere in what is the responsibility of the smaller communities and which they are in a position to do.

What is the purpose or objective of the State under the current Constitution?

According to article 1 of the current Constitution, "the State is at the service of the human person and its purpose is to promote the common good, for which it must contribute to creating the social conditions that will allow each and every one of the members of the national community their greatest possible spiritual and material realization., with full respect for the rights and guarantees established by this Constitution."

What does the Constitution say about pensions?

Pensions are the most important manifestation of the right to social security, recognized in article 19 N°18 of the current Constitution, which establishes the framework and general principles of this right. As with all social rights, they must be developed by the Executive and the Legislative Branches, which are responsible for implementing them and giving them substance. That is why the same article provides that the development of this right and the payment of contributions are matters that must be regulated by law, and that the State must "guarantee the access of all inhabitants to the enjoyment of uniform basic benefits, whether they are granted through public or private institutions". Examples: Law No. 21.190, which reformed the amounts of solidarity pensions; D.L. 3,500, which regulates the private pension system. However, at the end of July 2020, Congress passed a constitutional amendment to allow people to withdraw up to 10% of their pension funds, which, while a matter of law, was preferred to be regulated by a transitional constitutional rule.

What does the Constitution say about education?

The right to education is recognized in article 19 N°10 of the current Constitution, which establishes the framework and general principles of this right. As with all social rights, they must be developed by the Executive and the Legislative Branches, which are responsible for implementing them and giving them substance. This article recognizes the parents ' "the right of preference and the duty to educate their children", and imposes on the State the duty to "promote pre-school education, for which it shall finance a free system from the lower secondary level". It also provides for free and compulsory basic and secondary education, and the duty of the State to "promote the development of education at all levels; to stimulate scientific and technological research, artistic creation and the protection and enhancement of the nation's cultural heritage." Examples of education laws: General Education Law, No. 20,370; Law No. 21.091 on higher education, which establishes free higher education.

What does the Constitution say about health and the price of medicines?

The current Constitution recognizes the right to health protection in article 19 N°9 of the Constitution, which establishes the framework and general principles of this right. As with all social rights, they must be developed by the Executive and the Legislative Branches, which are responsible for implementing them and giving them substance. On the basis of this mandate, the Executive has carried out measures aimed at, for example, combating the Covid-19 pandemic, declaring the situation catastrophe, integrating the public and private health systems, improving hospital infrastructure and medical and health support, etc. For its part, access to medicines and their price is a matter that must be regulated by law. Examples: Law No. 20.850, which created a financial protection system for high-cost diagnoses and treatments (Ricarte Soto Law); Law No. 20.724, which amended the Health Code on the regulation of pharmacies and medicines (incorporates bioequivalents).

What does the Constitution say about salaries and salaries?

Wages and remuneration are the income to which the worker is entitled in return for the work freely chosen. The current Constitution recognizes freedom of work in article 19 No. 16, and provides that everyone has the right to a fair remuneration for his work, which must be agreed in the employment contract. However, it is the legislator who sets the minimum income annually, that is, the minimum remuneration that a worker must receive.

What does the Constitution say about property on highways and highways and on water?

Ownership of roads and water is regulated mostly in the Civil Code, and to a lesser extent in the Constitution. Thus, according to article 589 of the Civil Code, roads, streets and squares are owned by the State and are referred to as national property for public use. And article 595 of the same Code provides that all waters are the property of the State, and are therefore national assets for public use. However, article 19 N°24 of the Constitution says that people who have obtained a right to use water have ownership over this use. The right to use water is regulated in the Water Code.

There are many highlights of the constituent process and what surrounds it, after seeing all the information and content that this process carries, we have been able to understand the fundamental of a constitution that is to limit power. And for that every constitution must recognize all these named and enumerated points.

1. The rule of law: Both rulers and citizens subject to the law.

2. Supremacy of the constitution: The constitution is above power and the other rules that govern the country.

3. Separation of powers: No authority concentrates all power.

4. Fundamental rights: Faculties that we all have because we are human beings and that the rulers cannot violate.

A constitution that does not limit power cannot be called a constitution.

Nor can the constitution be expected to contain all the right. There are matters which will necessarily have to be regulated in greater detail in other rules. Example: details of electoral procedures, health and pension systems, etc. Constitutions that try to regulate everything in detail tend to be more unstable and end up being constantly modified.

Chapter 22

United States, Power and International Order

President Obama's inauguration marked the opening of a new chapter in U.S. foreign policy and U.S. relations with other states. The invasion of Iraq, the flouting of international conventions on torture, the treatment of prisoners of war, and opposition to a series of international treaties - legacies of the Bush administration - all seemed to show America acting separately. But whether the US, which possesses unparalleled military advantages but waning economic power, will be able to model renewed global leadership is far less clear. Even less obvious is what kind of power the U.S. would be in a changing international system.

In this course we examine the future of American power in the international order with an overview of some of the most important foreign policy challenges bequeathed by the Bush administration. We look at America's long-term project to create a liberal international order and some of the tensions that underlie it, and then explore the idea that America has a unique place in the international system by looking at the idea of "Americanism."

Having established some of these more general and conceptual ideas about American power in the international system, we evaluated America's ability to lead the same system by studying U.S. relations with other liberal powers and with the emerging powers of China and Russia, and U.S. policy with respect. to the Middle East and West Asia.

A world of problems

What some called a 'hell inbox' presented the Obama administration with an unenviable range of problems. However, many of these problems have been around for some time, and all U.S. presidents have to deal with multiple foreign policy challenges. What was different about the beginning of Obama's presidency was that it sought, so openly, to signal a turning point in U.S. foreign policy and to try to reposition America's place in the world. Indeed, it was a sign of how discredited Bush's foreign policy within the US had become that Democrats, so often susceptible to Republican taunts of being "soft" on security, should have been able to make this foreign policy stance one of the major electoral victories in 2008. Thus, while many of the key issues facing Obama were long-standing, even before the Bush administration, Obama's inauguration marked a moment in history when the U.S. government sought to shape a new beginning for American leadership. The brief and partial 'study' of some of the key aspects of the US foreign policy agenda. Below (and you could easily add to the list topics like the environment or the problems of American industry) is not intended to give you an idea of the problem. details of politics, which inevitably change over time, but rather to outline the main features of an America that sought to reshape its image and renew its leadership.

The wars started by the Bush administration in Iraq and Afghanistan were some of the most problematic issues facing the new administration. The new president took office promising a "definitive" end to the war in Iraq, an act that would also allow a refocus on the longer-running war in Afghanistan. For many, the Bush administration's diversion of military, political, and economic resources toward the invasion of Iraq in 2003, so soon after the invasion of Afghanistan in 2001, was one of its key strategic mistakes. The fact that this has been done without broad international support, UN backing or proper planning for the aftermath simply compounded the problems. Obama's initial Iraq policy reinforced a direction of travel that Bush had already reluctantly adopted. The violence and chaos in Iraq that began to spiral out of control in 2006 was due to an "increase" in the number of U.S. troops in 2007 and the courtship of the U.S. and Iraqi governments with opposition groups. In early 2009, President Obama announced plans for the withdrawal of troops from Iraq: a reduction to 50,000 by 2010 (below a maximum of 142,000 U.S. troops), and the rest departed under a security agreement with the Iraqi government by 2011.

Even with an optimistic view that this would be possible, an exit from Afghanistan seemed much more problematic. Bush had already announced an increase in the number of troops in Afghanistan, a move that Obama reinforced upon taking office. After a two-month review of the situation in Afghanistan and Pakistan, Obama announced a new package in March 2009. While many of the elements of the strategy were not entirely new, it represented an attempt to highlight the importance of the Afghan conflict. within U.S. foreign policy and a reinvigorated effort to reverse what many commentators saw as a worsening situation. In addition to more troops, the U.S. hoped to accelerate efforts to train and equip the Afghan military (the establishment of which was one of the few successes of the previous policy) and increase development aid.

However, U.S. policy also had to address the emerging link between the situation in Afghanistan and political change in Pakistan. The border areas between the two countries, and in particular Pakistan's tribal areas, had long been considered the source of support for the revitalized Taliban and al-Qaeda's main base of operations. Some commentators welcomed the development of a joint policy towards the two countries together. The Bush administration, in appreciation of Musharraf's support after September 11, had provided Pakistan's military with more than $11 billion in aid with few conditions. Instead, Obama made new disbursements of planned $1,500 million a year depending on Pakistan's government demonstrating progress in its fight against al-Qaeda and the Taliban inside Pakistan. Similarly, U.S. policy now aimed to condition cooperation with the Afghan central government on progress toward fighting rampant corruption. In part to address domestic U.S. political opposition, Obama also continued the attempt to persuade NATO allies to provide more troops and/or financial backing to the renewed effort in Afghanistan.

No less difficult on the agenda was the problem of nuclear proliferation, centered on the ambitions of Iran and North Korea. Both countries had come under criticism from the United States and the United Nations for their efforts to develop nuclear weapons and non-compliance (as many saw it) with the Nuclear Non-Proliferation Treaty (NPT). In both respects, however, except for military strikes, U.S. influence remains limited, and the obvious costs of taking military action inevitably make the threat of such action less credible. Moreover, other diplomatic pressures, such as sanctions or, in the case of North Korea, the promise of aid of various kinds, were limited without broad international support. Obama's initial policy on this issue was to try to establish a new position around which he hoped to galvanize more international support. He therefore reiterated the underlying principles of the NPT (whereby non-nuclear states would give up the acquisition of nuclear weapons in exchange for serious efforts by nuclear-weapon states to disarm) in calling for steps toward a non-nuclear world. And he called for a fresh start in relations with Iran on the basis of "tough diplomacy."

Crucial to any U.S. progress on this issue, however, is the support of China and Russia, both permanent members of the U.N. Security Council (and thus capable of blocking any U.N.-wide sanctions program), and both with a variety of close ties to Iran. and North Korea. Along with the prospect of Iran and North Korea developing nuclear forces, there was the permanent possibility that nuclear weapons or nuclear weapons material would fall into terrorist hands through political conflict or state collapse in other nuclear states.

Finally, the economic and financial crisis that emerged during 2007-2009 called into question elements of the liberal economic order that had been the centerpiece of America's relationship with other capitalist powers. Trying to deal with the crisis not only meant forging new forms of cooperation with major capitalist states by seeking to align government stimulus packages, central bank actions, and bank rescue agreements, but it also presented some new and unique problems for the United States:

1. Because the crisis hit the U.S. national economy so hard. And it came at a time when the U.S. Beset by other foreign policy issues detailed above, weakened the ability of the US. To set the terms of the response.

2. The emergence of new economic powers, particularly China and India, meant that negotiations to deal with the crisis had to take into account a much wider and more diverse range of states than had been the norm in economic affairs until then.

3. The very fact that the crisis was considered to have been 'made in the United States', since it was the US economy and the US approach to financial regulation that was at its heart, undermined the notion that the US economy is the leading economy in the world. As you will see later, American leadership of the capitalist world had relied heavily on this force.

What is perhaps most surprising about this range of problems is not that they have arisen all at once; that would be pretty difficult. It is that actions in one field have created obstacles to progress in others. America's ability to deal with the Afghan war is compounded by the reluctance of NATO allies to send additional troops, in part because of the divisions that opened up within the Western alliance as a result of Bush's Iraq policy. America's attempts to curtail Iran's and North Korea's nuclear ambitions are equally constrained by the limited cooperation it can forge with China and Russia. And that uncertainty also limits their ability to lead the response to the economic crisis.

International Order and American Dilemmas

We'll start thinking about these questions by considering at a very general level what the U.S. is trying to achieve in the international system.

What is the U.S.'s long-term goals for the international order?

To answer this question, we first need a practical definition of what the international order is. As you have already seen, there are different ways of understanding and characterizing the international order. Among these, three notions of international order underlie much of the discussion that follows here. The first, more closely associated with realism, but not only, is the idea that the international order is the product, in a system of anarchic states, of a balance of power: the coercive power of states (or the potential to use such power) is aligned against that of others. The order here is formed by the power of one controlling that of others, or of the strong dominating the week.

However, it has also seen that the international order can arise from interdependence and, in particular, from positive-sum forms of interdependence. Order here is a collective property of states that can coordinate some of their interactions for mutual benefit. The English School holds that the international order arises from "a sense of common interests in those elementary or primary goals [of social life]; by the rules that prescribe the pattern of behavior that sustains them; and by the institutions that give effect to these rules" (Bull, 1995 [1977], p. 51). For the English School, the main objectives of social life include guarantees of safety, agreements and property, and patterns of behavior that underpin them. For others, such as liberal analysts of the post-World War II international order, the pursuit of great absolute gains plays a crucial role in sustaining the particular patterns of behavior of a liberal international order. Finally, Marxist analyses of imperialism and hegemony in the international capitalist system seek to show how both power and interdependence are shaped by the unequal development of the capitalist world economy. In this course we take the view that the three notions - power, positive-sum interdependence, and capitalist development - play a role in a considered description of the United States in the international order. Marxist analyses of imperialism and hegemony in the capitalist international system seek to show how both power and interdependence are shaped by the unequal development of the capitalist world economy. In this course we take the view that the three notions - power, positive-sum interdependence, and capitalist development - play a role in a considered description of the United States in the international order. Marxist analyses of imperialism and hegemony in the capitalist international system seek to show how both power and interdependence are shaped by the unequal development of the capitalist world economy. In this course we take the view that the three notions - power, positive-sum interdependence, and capitalist development - play a role in a considered description of the United States in the international order.

So, what do the challenges described in the previous section tell us about America's ability to reshape the international order, whether by altering the balance of coercive power or pursuing mutual goals with other states? Indeed, together with a number of long-term trends, these problems help to raise with particularly acute prominence a central dilemma that American strategists have faced since the end of World War II: the fact that measures taken to strengthen the international system are in the interest of the United States., will inevitably strengthen its competitors and weaken its relative power. What do we mean by that?

On the one hand, a steady diffusion of economic power has been both an inevitable result of the processes of economic development brought about by the expansion of the capitalist world economy and an explicit guiding ambition of American foreign policy. That is, the United States has consistently sought to promote economic development, including, inevitably, recovery development by other states, in key parts of the rest of the capitalist world. This was precisely the intention of American efforts to rebuild Western Europe and Japan after World War II, for example. On the other hand, the effect of this long-term relative decline in America's economic leadership means that, as a result, the United States could not contain or limit a wider diffusion of political power. As an underlying overarching strategic reality, this paradox has provoked two main U.S. responses and a lingering tension within U.S. foreign policy.

One answer, no doubt, has been ted efforts to maintain military pre-eminence over other liberal powers and especially in relation to potential rivals outside the liberal core, as well as to sustain, as far as possible, the vitality of its own economy. Such efforts have been spurred by the need to make the United States "safe" from international threats and to protect the American "way of life" and domestic order from the outside. This impulse has been the basis of isolationist policy in the United States for some time.

But a different impulse has been to make the world "safe" for an America whose power is sure to diminish, as it seeks to transform the international order. This latter response sought to square the circle by ensuring America's security and way of life through a project to make the rest of the world more open to American values. From this perspective, the dominant one in U.S. foreign policy from World War II onwards, the U.S. international order project meant a project of economic expansion, diffusion and updating by other countries, and a political project of changing the internal characteristics of the United States. other leading states and, as far as possible, ensuring that other states' commitments to the international economic and political system were broadly liberal. Indeed, precisely because relative economic decline has been deemed inevitable, and that dominance will eventually pass, the imperative to transform the rest of the world into an American direction has been so strong. While Obama's statement that 'we reject as false the choice between our security and our ideals' spoke more obviously about the relationship between civil liberties and security, it can also be read as part of a broader and longer-lasting vision of America's strategic interests. For example, President Truman declared that the "American system" could only survive by becoming "a global system" (quoted in Fergusson, 2004, p.80); or as James Warburg said, American citizens "are willing to become citizens of the world, but only if this becomes an extension of the United States" (quoted in Prestowitz, 2003, p.117).

Americanism and empire

The United States claims an exceptional role in world affairs, uniquely defining its national interest as more or less synonymous with that of the international community as a whole. His liberal defenders agree: "America's national interest ... offers the closest correspondence that exists with a worldwide interest" (Emmott, 2002, p. 10). It is the only country with an 'ism' attached to its name (Prestowitz, 2003).

Why are the UNITED STATES claiming such an exceptional international role?

To answer this, we must go back to the historical development of the United States itself. The Formation of the U.S. It was the result of the networks of trade, people, settlements and ideas that circulated in the Atlantic economy, uniting northwestern Europe, the Americas and Africa during the seventeenth and eighteenth centuries. After thirteen colonies gained independence from Britain in the American Revolution of 1776, the further development of the U.S. It was partly an indirect continuation of that process of European expansion into the non-European world, both globalizing and imperial.

At the same time, however, American expansion was defined as anticolonial rather than colonial, republican rather than monarchical, the New World rather than the old European order. Unlike the major European states, the United States became a great power more or less without a formal empire. Rather, independence paved the way for westward expansion and settlement, and "the entire internal history of U.S. imperialism was a vast process of territorial takeover and occupation" (Stedman Jones, 1972, p. 217).

It was only by presenting this "internal colonialism" as an expansion into uninhabited or freely alienated lands that the American ideology of "exceptionalism" could take root. However, among the overwhelming Majority of The European population, such an idea struck a chord. The ideology of exceptionalism encompasses two sets of ideas:

1. That the United States is fortunate to have escaped the patterns of historical development characteristic of the old order in Europe and to be able to re-create a society based on security, freedom and justice.

2. That it is an exemplary power, representing a model universally applicable to the rest of humanity.

In this way, the United States has been able to present its national interest as unique and universal at the same time, as entirely consistent with a form of cosmopolitan internationalism.

The consolidation of Union sovereignty after the Civil War of 1861-1865 and the development of the domestic market, based on federal transfers of land to private property, laid the foundation for the further development of a mass society: the United States pioneered the culture of mass consumption as well as the consumption of mass culture, both based on mass production, or what foreigners simply called Americanism.

Americanism. Americanism refers to the combination of mass production, a culture of mass consumption, and mass consumption of culture promoted by American capitalist society.

The fact that the US has exerted such influence, through attraction and imitation, as well as through military dominance and "tools of control", has led to a long-standing debate about whether the US. It's an imperial country and in what way. energy. This remains a crucial issue. As you will see, in a context of relative economic decline, different conceptions of imperialism and inter-imperialist relations carry very different forecasts for the future of U.S. power. So, let's start by expounding some ideas about what "imperialism" means.

What does the term ' imperialism ' or ' empire' mean?

Perhaps the most general way in which the term "empire" has been used is an idea, originally derived from the Roman Empire and the impact of Greek and Christian cultures, of empire as a hierarchy of political entities producing a universal order based on shared criteria. identities, values and interests, in which one power, the imperial or hegemonic, rises above the others. This is a notion of empire as "first and foremost, a great power that has left its mark on the international relations of its time" (Lieven, 2003, p. XIV). Empire as a form of government (not necessarily a direct government) over many territories and peoples, generally associated with an economic and cultural order that proclaims itself as the basis of a universal civilization. No such empire has ever been truly universal. However, this is a way of thinking about the American empire in the early twenty-first century. A key question for this idea of an American empire is, "How does the United States leave its mark on the international relations of its time?"

In the modern era, attempts to define empire have been reported by Marxist and radical liberal thinkers who have tried to understand the character of European colonial empires. These focused on the nature of the competitive relationship between rival national imperialisms that, in combination, dominated the non-European world until decolonization. "Empire" can be used in the "narrow" sense of the formal political subordination of one political entity to another, the clearest example being the discussion of colonialism. And, in fact, for John Hobson, the radical liberal critic and analyst of the British Empire, this alludes to one aspect of empire. But Hobson drew a distinction between what he called "imperialism" by which he referred to political relations between states, and the "informal empire." Giovanni Aright explains this distinction as follows:

At least in principle ... two quite different types of rivalry were involved. In the case of imperialism, rivalry affected political relations between states and was expressed in the arms race and the drive for territorial expansion; while, in the case of the Informal Empire, it referred to economic relations between individuals of different nationalities and was expressed in the international division of work. Thus, imperialism meant political conflict between nations, economic interdependence of the informal Empire between them.

(Arrighi, 1983, p. 41)

CHAPTER 23

Trade war

Former President Donald Trump instituted a protectionist trade policy, one of the great economic objectives that most attracts president Trump's attention is the trade deficit. In other words, Trump seeks to correct the negative difference between exports and imports. Obviously, to achieve this goal Trump had two options: one option is to stimulate the export of domestic products, while the second alternative is to reduce imports of foreign products.

Well, Trump, try or hinder the entry of Chinese products, has opted for tariffs, that is, to establish taxes that make foreign goods more expensive. On the other hand, Trump believes that by setting tariffs, he will succeed in boosting and protecting the U.S. steel and aluminum industries. The U.S. government wants to curb Chinese power in the steel sector, because China, as the world's largest steel producer, has a significant surplus that it can export at prices so low that U.S. companies cannot compete.

The big one affected by this policy would be China. And the government reported that the new tariffs that the Asian giant will have to bear will amount to about 60,000 million dollars.

With barriese, Chínese products will become more expensive and will no longer be as competitive in the U.S. market, hence in China they are upset with the protectionist trade policy of the U.S. government.

So, these new tariffs seem to be the classic starting gun for a trade war. Such wars begin with a country's decision to establish tariffs or any other type of barriers to free trade. In this case, the US Administration seems to have lit the fuse of the conflict. In response, the country harmed by trade barriers will counterattack with measures such as new tariffs, quotas, administrative obstacles. In this sense, the Chinese have a whole arsenal at their disposal, with nothing more and nothing less than the imposition of tariffs on 128 American products. For the time being, the Chinese response has remained a warning, but if the situation worsens, the consequences may be harsh for international trade and for the population.

To begin with, we must talk about the benefits of free trade that were generated in the last years of the twentieth century and the beginning of the twenty-first century, which favored the growth of the international economy and the well-being of the world's population in general.

Economic globalization reached levels never seen before. The world's consumers were able to obtain an ever-greater variety of products with the best quality characteristics and the best prices in international competition.

In the same way, companies from all countries of the world found the doors open to a global market where they could place their products in the place in the world where it will be most convenient for them.

It happens that after the great crisis of 2008, where the most developed countries of the world suffered the impact of low or no growth of the gross domestic product (GDP),an increase in the level of unemployment, a recessionary process and with negative trade balances; they began to apply monetary, fiscal and trade policies to achieve a reactivation of their economies.

In the case of international trade, protectionist barriers or policies began to be applied to protect their trade balances and their domestic producers. This situation has hardened more between 2018 and 2019 and especially among the great powers such as the United States and China.

We can say that taxes increase the price of products and that over price is always paid by the consumer

The positive scenario would only be achieved in the short term, but in the long term we will most likely experience the negative scenario. Protections of any kind to the trade balance or as in the case of Trump's veto for Huawei only make companies less competitive and reduce trade and GDP growth globally.

But what about the new US administration?

The U.S. president decided to ban U.S. investments in a dozen Chinese technology and defense companies with alleged military ties.
The new executive order, which the White House reported this week, takes effect on August 2 and will affect 59 firms in the Asian

country, including giant Huawei and the nation's three largest telecommunications companies.

It is an extension of the order previously signed by his predecessor, Donald Trump, which promoted a hardening of the stance with China and led some experts to warn of a "new cold war."

The decree expands the scope of another executive order signed last November by former President Trump that vetoed the country's investments in some thirty Chinese companies for allegedly supporting the efforts of Beijing's intelligence, military and security apparatuses.

The goal of the veto is to ensure that U.S. investments "do not support the Chinese defense sector," Biden's White House explained.

bibliography

Declarations of the rights of man and citizen 1879. Available in: https://www.conseilconstitutionnel.fr/sites/default/files/as/root/bank_mm/espagnol/es_ddhc.pdf

The United States Constitution of 1787. available in: https://www.archives.gov/espanol/constitucion

In Congress, July 4, 1776, a declaration of the representatives of the United States of America was assembled in the General Congress. Available in: https://www.loc.gov/resource/rbc0001.2004pe76546/

It establishes the consolidated, coordinated and systematized text of the political constitution of the Republic of Chile. Available in: https://www.bcn.cl/leychile/navegar?idNorma=242302

undp_cl_gobernabilidad_INFORME_Mecanismos_cambio_constitucional.

Legal principles and legal system. Bases for a general theory of legal principles in the Chilean constitutional system. Available in: https://derechoyhumanidades.uchile.cl/index.php/RDH/article/view/34821

Constitution under discussion. available in: https://uabierta.uchile.cl/courses/course-v1:Universidad_de_Chile+UCH_38+2019/about

Conditions for democracy (Robert Dahl). available at: https://politicaymedios.net/condiciones-para-la-democracia/

Parties, movements and coalitions. Available in: https://www.bcn.cl/historiapolitica/partidos_politicos/periodo?per=1833-1891

political party. available in: http://sil.gobernacion.gob.mx/Glosario/definicionpop.php?ID=178

Parties constituted. Available in: https://www.servel.cl/partidos-constituidos/?mla_paginate_current=2

Welcome to the Chile law. Available in: https://www.bcn.cl/leychile/

What is politics for? Available in: https://elpais.com/diario/2004/01/20/paisvasco/1074631203_850215.html

Guide to civic formation - the State. Available in: https://www.bcn.cl/formacioncivica/detalle_guia?h=10221.3/45681

Political system. Available in: https://chile.gob.cl/chile/sistema-politico

Interests of chile's foreign policy. Available in: https://minrel.gob.cl/minrel/politica-exterior/intereses-de-la-politica-exterior-de-chile#:~:text=La%20pol%C3%ADtica%20exterior%20search%20project us,%20exports%20of%20bienes%20y foreign policy. Available in: https://chile.gob.cl/chile/politica-exterior

Principle of the foreign policy of Chile. Available in: https://www.minrel.gob.cl/minrel/politica-exterior/principios-de-la-politica-exterior-chilena

economy. Available in: https://chile.gob.cl/chile/economia#:~:text=Chile%20es%20a%20pa%C3%ADs%20abierto,otros%20pa%C3%ADses%20y%20bloques%20comercials.&text=Adem%C3%A1s%2C%20en%20marzo%20del%202007,el%2087%25%20del%20PIB%20mundial

-The Political Economy of British Columbia's Rainforests by Elmer G. Wiens

Political economy station

New Chilean electoral system: D'Hondtmethod. Available in: https://www.servel.cl/nuevo-sistema-electoral-chileno-metodo-dhont-2/

-Hanna Arendt, p. 68.

The action as revelation of the agent in Hanna Arendt: identity gesture and crisis of representation. Available in: https://eprints.ucm.es/id/eprint/35921/

- Machiavelli Nicholas, the prince, ed. various, chapter XV.

- Machiavelli Nicholas, the Prince, ed. various, chapter XVII.

- Weber Max, economics and society, economic culture fund, pp. 1043-1076.

- The Federalist, various editions.

- Aristotle, miscellaneous editions, politics.

- Max Weber, science and politics, "politics as a profession", ed. Miscellaneous.

- Article 63 of the Constitution), and the courts to dispense justice (article 76 of the Constitution.

- Münch Galindo & García Martínez, 1990.

Anderson, P. (2002) 'Force and consent', *New Left Review II* , n. ° 17, pp. 5-30.

Arrighi, G. (1983) *The Geometry of Imperialism* (revised edition), London, Verse.

Baran, P. & Sweezy, P. (1966) *Monopoly capital* , Harmondsworth, Penguin.

Bright, C. & Meyer, M. (2002) 'Where in the world is America? The History of the U.S. In the Global Era ' in Bender, T. (ed.) *Rethinking American History in a Global Age* , Berkeley, CA, University of California Press.

Bull, H. (1995 [1977]) *The Anarchical Society* (second edition), London, Macmillan.

Bullion, A. (2007) *Sri Lanka: Special issue of Civil Wars* , Abingdon, Taylor and Francis.

Burke, J. (2003) *Al-Qaeda: Casting a Shadow of Terror* , New York, IB Tauris

Burke, J. (2004) *Al-Qaeda* , Harmondsworth, Penguin.

Buzan, B. (2004) *The United States and the Great Powers* , Cambridge, Polity Press.

Emmott, B. (2002) 'Present at the creation', *The Economist,* 29 June.

Fergusson, N. (2004) *Colossus* , London, Allen Lane.

Fox, WTR (1944) *The Superpowers* , New York, Harcourt, Brace, Jovanovich.

Goldstein, A. (2001) 'The Diplomatic Face of China's Grand *Strategy', China Quarterly,* vol.168.

Gramsci, A. (1971) *Selections from Prison Notebooks of Antonio Gramsci* (edited and translated by Hoare, Q. and Nowell Smith, G.), London, Lawrence and Wishart.

Halliday, F. (2002) *Two hours that shook the world. September 11, 2001: Causes and consequences* , London, Saqi Books.

Hausmann, R., Lim, E. and Spence, A. (2006) 'China and the global economy: medium-term issues and options - a Synthesis report', Harvard University, KSG Working paper No. RWP06-029, China and the Economy global ; [Accessed 25 July 2009].

Hull, C. (2004) in Brown, W., Bromley, S. and Athreye, S. (Eds) *Ordering the International: History, Change and Transformation (A World of Whose Making?)* , London, Pluto Press.

Ignatieff, M. (2003) *Empire Lite* , London, Vintage.

Kant, I. (1991; first published in 1795) 'Perpetual Peace: A Philosophical Sketch' in Reiss, H. (ed.) *Kant: Political Writings* (second edition), Cambridge, Cambridge University Press.

Kautsky, K. (1970; first published in 1914) ' Ultraimperialism ', *New Left Review I* , no 59, pp. 41-6.

Klare, M. (2003) *Blood and Oil* , London, Hamish Hamilton.

Lenin, VI (1916) *Imperialism, the highest stage of capitalism* , Beijing, Foreign Language Press.

Lieven, D. (2003) *Empire* , London, Pimlico.

Mearsheimer, J. (2001) *The Tragedy of Great Power Politics* , New York, WW Norton and Co.

Obama, B (2009) Inauguration Speech, Washington, DC, January 2009 [Online], <u>Obama Inauguration</u> [Accessed July 24, 2009].

Prestowitz, C. (2003) *Rogue Nation* , New York, Basic Books.

Rashid, A. (2001) *Taliban* , London, Pan Macmillan.

Rashid, A. (2009) 'Pakistan on the brink', *New York Review* , May 23.

Stedman Jones, G. (1972) 'The History of U.S. Imperialism' in Blackburn, R. (ed.) *Ideology in Social Science: Readings in Critical Social Theory* , Glasgow, Fontana / Collins.

9 798544 197638